# HEALTH-RELATED RESOURCES FOR BLACK AND MINORITY ETHNIC GROUPS

## Second edition

HPiC

**Acknowledgements**

The Health Education Authority would like to thank all those who have contributed to the development of the first and second editions of this database publication, including all those who have made resources available for review.

In particular, the HEA thanks the reviewers and critical readers, listed in Appendix 1.

Thanks also to the project teams at the HEA, especially Mary Ryan, Chandy Perera, Katherine Vik, Claudette Edwards, Victoria Fitch, Heidi Livingstone and Frances Bird (Project Manager).

First edition 1994
Second edition 1999

© Health Education Authority 1999

Health Education Authority
Trevelyan House
30 Great Peter Street
London SW1P 2HW

www.hea.org.uk

Cover design by Tanya Field
Typeset by Type Generation
Printed in Great Britain

ISBN 0 7521 1167 1

# Contents

# Foreword

Providing high quality and equitable health information and advice to an increasingly diverse nation is one of the supremely difficult yet noble goals facing the health sector. This resource, a welcome second edition, records that many individuals and agencies are striving and succeeding in achieving the goal. As a database, this work is invaluable. For those already familiar with the field, the database will reduce the need to reinvent the wheel. For newcomers to health promotion, finding this resource is essentially discovering the wheel.

The database also serves a longer term, and ultimately more important role – to remind us of what we still need to do, so that future databases will be even richer in resources.

The database shows that needs are still being met in a fragmentary way, without a master plan or strategy. The individualism shines through. The needs being met reflect local and individual perceptions. Some population groups are better served than others are – for example, the Chinese population remains inadequately served.

The development of key materials is still often left to voluntary agencies and the commercial sector (the main listed resource for tackling the titanic problem of coronary heart disease in South Asians is produced by a drug company). The costs of videos are high in relation to their length. Mass production and distribution is needed to slash costs, but this can only be done by central intervention. For key topics there may be a need for a video in every home. With costs of £20–40 per video, this cannot be achieved on current approaches.

In this busy, overstretched decentralised decade, the Health Education Authority's (HEA's) database demonstrates advances, but identifies much work for the new millennium. As with all major challenges a well equipped, expertly trained workforce, building on the collective past experience and working to a detailed strategy, is most likely to succeed. Scarce expertise will need to be more carefully nurtured and directed than hitherto, and fresh thinking will be required. Organisations such as the HEA will be needed to continue to lead, to harness and demonstrate the achievements of the many dedicated people across the UK, and to focus us on the tasks ahead.

**Raj Bhopal**
Bruce and John Usher Chair of Public Health
Professor of Public Health, Edinburgh University

# Introduction

This book is the revised edition of the original publication, *Health-Related Resources for Black and Minority Ethnic Groups*, produced by the Health Education Authority (HEA) in 1994. The publication informs those involved in commissioning, purchasing or providing health care services for black and minority ethnic groups about the range of health-related resources available.

The information is also available on the national database for health promotion in the Health Promotion Information Centre (HPiC) at the HEA. The database is updated regularly and this publication includes those resources added to the database since it was established in 1994.

The health-related resources database for black and minority ethnic groups was the first of a series of health-related resources databases developed by the HPiC. These provide a comprehensive source of information about resources that can be used to promote health and healthy lifestyles, and access to health services. The databases, commissioned by the Department of Health, are targeted at population groups that are traditionally hard-to-reach, have particular health needs, or for whom it is difficult to find appropriate resources.

To date, the database series includes health-related resources for:

- Black and minority ethnic groups.
- People with learning disabilities.
- Older people.
- Young people (11–19 years old).
- Men.

## Background

Since the early 1990s and the publication in 1994 of *Health-Related Resources for Black and Minority Ethnic Groups* there have been many changes within the National Health Service (NHS) and in community care services. Government policy and directives have emphasised the importance of needs assessment, effectiveness in treatment and prevention, access to services, and greater involvement by service users. Increasingly, the needs of specific population groups have been highlighted, in particular the health needs of black and minority ethnic groups. As the Chief Medical Officer's report concluded in 1991, 'people working within the health service need to be aware of the differences, both in terms of disease patterns and lifestyle, and to consider how these differences need to inform appropriate service provision.'[1]

Black and minority ethnic groups represent six per cent of the population of the UK (3.4 million). Among some groups there is a higher proportion of young people compared to the majority (white) population. Black and minority ethnic groups in the UK encompass a wide range of communities with diverse cultures. This diversity is reflected in their language, religion and way of life.

The health status, beliefs and lifestyles of black and minority ethnic groups also differ and there are significant health variations and inequalities among this population. Since the early 1990s a growing number of studies and reports have highlighted these differences. *Ethnicity and Health. A Guide for the NHS*[2] was written to inform purchasing authorities of the health status and needs of minority ethnic groups to ensure the provision of appropriate health promotion and treatment services. As well as highlighting variations in mortality and morbidity among minority ethnic groups, the guide also noted that the aetiology and causation of certain conditions may be different. This has implications for the design and delivery of treatment services and health promotion interventions with this audience.

Produced in support of the government health strategy at that time, *The Health of the Nation*[3], *Ethnicity and Health* focused on the five priority areas for health improvement: coronary heart disease (CHD) and stroke; cancers; mental illness; HIV/AIDS and sexual health; and accidents. In the majority of these areas, the available epidemiological evidence shows that black and minority ethnic groups are at greater risk[2,4]. The guide also flagged up other areas of priority for the health of black and minority ethnic groups, including diabetes, infant health, haemoglobinopathies and access to health care. Among the recommendations made in the guide was a call for the development of appropriate preventive measures and educational campaigns, and the provision of appropriate primary and secondary care services that are sensitive to the needs of black and minority ethnic groups. This publication can assist those engaged in primary prevention services by highlighting health-related resources that can be used with different audiences.

The implementation of *The Health of the Nation* strategy included the establishment of a series of task forces, including the Black and Ethnic Health Task Force. On the recommendation of this task force, the NHS Ethnic Health Unit (NHS EHU) was established in 1994 for a period of three years. The purpose of the Unit was to assist the NHS to meet the health needs of black and minority ethnic people, travellers and refugees in England.

Between 1994 and 1997, the NHS EHU supported local action, collaborated with key national organisations, and disseminated information about ethnic health and health variations. In particular, the NHS EHU sought to share information nationally within the NHS, improve access to primary health care, involve black and minority ethnic groups in the decision-making process of the health service, and encourage ethnic monitoring for the purpose of planning and service provision. A number of documents were published promoting good practice and effectiveness in the area of ethnic health and these are listed on page 20. Details of projects funded by the EHU together with other black and minority ethnic health initiatives can be found in a series of Directories produced by the NHS EHU and the Department of Health (see Appendix 2).

Since 1993, when the lack of epidemiological and research data about black and minority ethnic health was highlighted[2], several major studies have been undertaken. The HEA's *Black and Minority Ethnic Groups Health and Lifestyles Survey* (1995)[5] was the first national survey of knowledge, attitudes, behaviour and health status of this population, and complemented existing surveys targeted at the general population. It explored the range of factors that contribute towards the health status of African–Caribbeans, Bangladeshis, Indians/East African Asians, Pakistanis and Black Africans and assessed their health needs. The second black and minority ethnic groups survey focused on nutrition and physical activity and was published in October 1999[6].

More recently, the HEA published a qualitative research study into the health beliefs of the Chinese community in England (1998)[7]. Through individual interviews and focus groups, the study explores social representations of health and illness and their affect on health-related practices, examines the impact of lay knowledge on acquisition and use of new information, and identifies the main concerns associated with the experience and use of health services in England. This research will inform the HEA's third national black and minority ethnic health and lifestyle survey, which focuses on the Chinese population.

Other major surveys since the mid-1990s include the Policy Studies Institute surveys and the forthcoming annual Health Survey for England (1999). The latter will provide information about the prevalence of specific health conditions and about lifestyle patterns and will highlight differences in health status among black and minority ethnic groups in England.

A change of government in 1997 precipitated further developments within the NHS and in the national strategy for health in England. The consultation document, *Our Healthier Nation* (1998)[8] sets out a contract for health between the government, local services and communities, and individuals. In contrast to the more individual focus of the previous strategy, *Our Healthier Nation* stresses the need to tackle the underlying causes of health inequalities through economic and social policy. The government aims to narrow the health gap by prioritising the health of the worst off in society, the vulnerable and those excluded. Inevitably, this will include certain sections of the country's black and minority ethnic population who experience high unemployment, low incomes and poor housing. Black and minority ethnic groups face additional barriers to inclusion as a result of discrimination, language and cultural differences.

In announcing funding for eight new pilot projects to improve ethnic minority health, the Minister for Public Health said, 'Ensuring effective access to health services for people from black and minority ethnic groups is an important part of our programme to reduce social exclusion and inequalities in health provision'[9].

As with the previous health strategy, *Our Healthier Nation* gives priority to:

- Heart disease and stroke.
- Accidents.
- Cancer.
- Mental health.

The Acheson Report (1998)[10] has given a further impetus to the government's programme to tackle health inequalities. This report recommends that all government policies likely to have a direct or indirect effect on health should be evaluated in terms of their impact on health inequalities and should be formulated in such a way that favours the less well off. The report specifically emphasises the needs of minority ethnic groups in the development and implementation of policies aimed at reducing socio-economic inequalities. It also recommends the further development of services that are sensitive to the needs of minority ethnic people and that promote greater awareness of their health risks. To do this, the report suggests that black and minority ethnic groups are specifically considered in needs assessment, resource allocation, healthcare planning and provision. This includes the consideration of alternative methods of focusing resources for health promotion and public health care to reduce inequalities in health.

Whilst the government's role is to ensure that economic and social policy takes account of the needs of the most disadvantaged, health and local authorities are charged with planning and delivering services that meet the needs of local communities, in particular the needs of vulnerable groups. Health authorities are specifically required to take the lead and involve the public in the development of Health Improvement Programmes and Primary Care Groups. There is a strong emphasis on partnerships between health and local authorities and local communities to translate the national contract into community-based action.

Many localities have applied for and received funding through initiatives such as health action zones and the Primary Care Act pilots. Among these are a number of areas with large black and minority ethnic group populations. Some are targeting issues of priority for black and minority ethnic health, such as diabetes[11], and others are targeting specific groups, for example young people from black and minority ethnic groups and Asian women[12].

As communities become involved in defining their health needs and taking action, there will be an increasing demand for information and support to deliver this. Health promotion can play a role by helping to identify needs in the community and by supporting community action through training, peer education, community development, and improving access to health information and services. Health-related resources that are developed and evaluated with black and minority ethnic groups offer one means of engaging in direct health-related work with this audience. This publication and the database for black and minority ethnic groups enables professionals and people from black and minority ethnic groups to find out about resources covering a wide range of topics and which are targeted at diverse communities.

The following sections describe the project and how health-related resources for black and minority ethnic groups have developed throughout the 1990s.


# The project

As the national centre for health promotion information and advice in England, the HPiC supports and develops the capacity for effective health promotion at local and national level.

The health-related resources database project is one of several services designed to support local health promotion.

The database helps professionals who work with black and minority ethnic groups to identify and select appropriate resources for use with this audience. It also assists commissioners of services and those who produce health-related resources by highlighting gaps in provision.

The aims of the database are to:

- provide up-to-date information about current resources that promote health and healthy lifestyles, and access to health and community services;
- highlight gaps in the provision of resources.

# Original development

In the early 1990s, the HEA's Information Centre received numerous inquiries about health-related resources for black and minority ethnic groups. At the same time, the HEA was engaged in disseminating a range of Department of Health funded resources for this audience. At a series of national viewing days organised around the country in partnership with regional and district health authorities, it became clear that professionals were experiencing difficulties when trying to identify and select appropriate resources for use with black and minority ethnic groups.

As a result the HEA undertook a national search to identify as many health-related resources for this audience as possible. In 1993 over 4000 letters were sent out explaining the purpose of the project and requesting information. These were sent to a wide range of statutory and voluntary services in England concerned with health, including:

- health promotion departments;
- voluntary and community groups concerned with health;
- directors of public health;
- district dental officers;
- district specialists in community medicine;
- community dietitians;
- primary healthcare facilitators;
- environmental health officers;
- HIV/AIDS co-ordinators;
- directors of education;
- directors of social services;
- producers and distributors of health promotion resources;
- professional organisations concerned with health.

Information about the project was also included in a number of publications and newsletters. Over 800 written responses were received. These ranged from 'no information to share' through to catalogues and database printouts. The HEA also received a large number of phone calls from those wanting information and requesting searches for resources on particular topics or in specific languages. Many of those who responded in writing also requested a copy of the completed database.

The responses themselves were interesting. Various health promotion agencies sent in their own resource catalogues. Some held few resources for black and minority ethnic groups, and sometimes the resources were quite dated. Other health promotion agencies replied that they had no need of such resources because there were few black and minority ethnic groups in their locality. Several agencies, particularly those in areas with large numbers of people from different communities, were well supplied and some were involved in producing their own resources, often working with the target communities. However, other agencies, even those in areas with large black and minority ethnic populations, did not appear to be meeting the needs of these groups proactively; as one deputy district health promotion officer responded, 'We have never had any requests for such materials'.

Over 90 new resources and 19 forthcoming resources were identified as a result of the search. These were reviewed and included in the original publication and entered on the HPiC's database.

A number of criteria were established for inclusion in the database. Resources were included if they:

- could be used with the audience to educate about health and healthy lifestyles, health services and how to use them, or particular conditions and diseases;
- could be used to assist health professionals in assessing the needs of black and minority ethnic groups and how to meet those needs appropriately;
- were nationally available for sale or hire;
- were not more than five years old (older resources were included if they were of particular significance or quality).

# Critical readers

In order to ensure that the reviews were useful a number of people were asked to comment critically on several pilot reviews. These critical readers represented a wide range of health interests, skills and experience. They were asked to read and comment on a review of a resource with which they were familiar and a review of a resource completely new to them. A questionnaire was provided for this purpose. The readers found the reviews useful and suggested some minor changes. These were incorporated into the review structure.

A list of the critical readers can be found in Appendix 1.

# Continued development of the database

Since the database was developed in 1994, information staff at the HPiC have continued to identify and add resources to the database by scanning relevant journals, catalogues, and promotional material. Many producers of resources automatically send information about new materials to the HPiC. In 1998, a smaller scale search was conducted via key organisations and journals. Reviews of the resources are loaded onto the national database for health promotion, HealthProm*is*, in the HPiC. This can be accessed directly on the web at http://healthpromis.hea.org.uk or via http://www.hea.org.uk/hpic/index.html the HPiC pages on the HEA's main website.

This publication is the revised edition of the original published directory. The criteria for inclusion remain the same except that as more resources are produced for direct use with black and minority ethnic groups, inclusion is confined to these resources. Materials specifically for professional development purposes are not included in this publication although information about these can be searched on the HealthProm*is* database. Where resources are primarily for health professionals but include some guidance or advice around practical work with black and minority ethnic groups these are included.

Only resources produced from 1993 onwards are included in this publication to ensure that the information is current. There are 18 resources from the original publication retained in this edition. Resources produced prior to 1993 that were included in the original publication and that are still available remain on the HealthProm*is* database in the HPiC.

Some 85 additional resources are included in this publication. Comparing this number identified over the four years since 1994 with the 100 identified over an eight-year period for inclusion in the original publication, it is clear that more health-related resources are being developed for black and minority ethnic groups. Given that the 85 new resources exclude those aimed at professionals, then the total number of resources added to the database since 1994 is substantially more.

# Terminology

In this publication, the term 'black and minority ethnic groups' is used. The HEA acknowledges that the use of any term to describe the wide range of ethnic groups in the UK is sensitive. However, this term is intended to convey a common experience of discrimination and inequality among people whose skin colour is not white. There is no intention to cause offence to those who find this term unsatisfactory or who prefer not to include themselves in such a description. Increasingly, individuals are defining their own ethnicity and this calls into question the basis on which organisations assess ethnic origin.

More specifically, the HEA uses the term African–Caribbean to describe people who were born in or who have recent family origins in the Caribbean and who have distant family origins in Africa.

The term 'South Asian' is used to describe people from the Indian sub-continent, those who originated from India, Bangladesh and Pakistan.

The term 'health professional' is used throughout to describe anyone who may be involved in providing health care in a professional capacity including health promotion activities within the voluntary and statutory sectors.

The term 'resources' is used to describe a variety of formats. Many of these are available in community languages. The formats include videos, audio-cassettes, manuals and guides, booklets and training packs. The original publication included posters and models. Whilst these can be useful in health-related work with black and minority ethnic groups they are not included in this revised edition. Leaflets are also excluded because like posters they are often locally produced and have a shorter shelf-life. This makes them unsuitable for inclusion in this database. Information about leaflets can be obtained from local health promotion units and agencies, and national charities.

Items such as medical text books, journal articles, local reports and theses are excluded because the focus is on resources that have a practical application to health promotion activity rather than items that provide background reading or specialist medical information. However, the HealthProm*is* database can be searched for the latest key studies, documents, reports, surveys, books and journal articles on black and minority ethnic health. A list of key documents can be found on page 20 of this publication.

# What the original search revealed and trends since 1994

All the resources in this publication are available nationally so these findings do not reflect the volume of local material available. The resources identified in the original HEA search and subsequent updating are varied in terms of health topics covered and the communities addressed.

Prior to the HEA search in 1993, two other reviews of health promotion resources for black and minority ethnic groups were conducted. These provide a useful historical perspective and demonstrate a number of trends. Bhopal and Donaldson (1988)[13] analysed health promotion resources, including leaflets, between 1977 and 1987. They found that during this 10-year period 'the priorities for health education were birth control, pregnancy and child care'. They noted a lack of resources addressing topics such as prevention of chronic diseases, smoking and alcohol education.

The findings of Bhopal and Donaldson were then compared by Bhatt and Dickinson (1992)[14] with the resource lists, *Health Education for Ethnic Minorities*, produced by the Health Education Authority in 1987 and 1990. Bhatt and Dickinson noted that a wider range of resources were available covering areas such as women's health, use of health services, 'heart health', HIV and AIDS, and provision for carers. The absence of any resources relating to hypertension was noted with concern. There was little provision for African–Caribbean or Chinese communities.

It is difficult to compare the results of the 1993 search directly with the subsequent updating because resources for professionals are excluded and the topic categories have been amended. Nevertheless a number of trends are apparent. In 1993, the search found that more resources were produced for Bengali-speaking communities than any other, followed by Gujarati-, Punjabi-, Urdu- and Hindi-speaking communities respectively. This remains the case, although provision is more equal across the five Indian sub-continent languages/communities (Table 1). In the original publication it was suggested that the reason for this, whilst not clear, was possibly due to the production of a large number of resources by a few producers who specialised in the production of health resources for local Bengali-speaking communities.

Since Bhatt and Dickinson's analysis, the number of resources targeting Chinese communities has increased, closely followed by the number of resources for Vietnamese communities. However, the total number and the topic coverage for each community remains small compared to the number, range and quality of those produced for the majority (white) population.

Although African–Caribbean communities are the second largest ethnic population in the UK, the number of resources identified in 1993 for these communities did not reflect this. Among the reasons suggested for this, was the fact that because people from African–Caribbean communities speak English they are deemed to be served by resources produced for the majority population. In particular, the more recent trend towards resources designed to reflect and appeal to a multiracial and multicultural community might be seen as sufficient to meet the needs of the African–Caribbean communities. As the original publication noted, the effectiveness of these resources as opposed to the effectiveness of resources developed to target African–Caribbean communities directly has not been tested. Since 1994, however, there has been an increase in the number of resources targeted specifically at African–Caribbean and African communities in the UK.

The number of resources targeted at other languages and communities remains small. These include resources in Turkish, Greek, Arabic, Somali and Yemeni, plus resources for travellers. Since 1994, a multi-lingual resource, including the main European languages, has been added.

*Table 1. Number of resources available by languages/communities*

| Language/Community | Number |
| --- | :---: |
| African | 9 |
| African–Caribbean | 13 |
| Arabic | 7 |
| Bengali (including Sylheti) | 38 |
| Chinese (Cantonese speaking) | 14 |
| Farsi | 1 |
| French | 3 |
| German | 1 |
| Greek | 4 |
| Gujarati | 30 |
| Hindi | 26 |
| Italian | 1 |
| Mirpuri | 2 |
| Polish | 2 |
| Punjabi | 31 |
| Pushto | 1 |
| Somali | 10 |
| Spanish | 1 |
| Tamil | 1 |
| Travellers | 2 |
| Turkish | 10 |
| Urdu | 34 |
| Vietnamese | 5 |
| Welsh | 1 |
| Yemeni | 1 |

*Note:* This table includes those resources produced in languages other than English, and those resources specifically targeted at certain communities. Several resources produced in English are aimed generally at a range of communities and are not included in this list. Some resources are counted more than once as they are available in several languages.

Table 2, opposite, refers to the health topics covered by the resources in this updated publication. Resources may appear under several topics. The list of topics has been amended since the original publication in order to standardise the categories across the various health-related resources databases, and to bring it into line with the Health Promotion Thesaurus terms used in the HPiC.

*Table 2. Number of resources by topic*

| Topics | Number |
|---|---|
| Access to health services | 10 |
| Access to community services | 3 |
| Advocacy | 2 |
| Alcohol | 6 |
| Ante- and postnatal care | 6 |
| Child health | 4 |
| Communication | 7 |
| Drugs and solvent misuse | 2 |
| Education | 3 |
| Environment | 1 |
| Equal Opportunities | 13 |
| Health conditions and illnesses | 23 |
| Immunisation | 1 |
| Infant feeding | 4 |
| Mental health | 2 |
| Nutrition | 18 |
| Older people | 1 |
| Oral health | 3 |
| Parenting | 2 |
| Physical activity | 2 |
| Professional education and development | 3 |
| Religion | 2 |
| Safety | 2 |
| Screening | 5 |
| Sexual health and personal relationships | 12 |
| Smoking | 6 |
| Travellers | 2 |
| Women's health | 14 |
| Work and the workplace | 1 |

*Note:* Resources may appear under several topics.

In the original 1994 publication, a significant development was the increase in resources relating to professional development. Many of these aimed to inform health professionals about different communities, their health needs and how to work appropriately with people from different communities. Resources about cultural identity, access to health services and communication also increased. This probably reflected the growing emphasis on improving service provision and access to services for black and minority ethnic groups[2]. This revised edition does not include resources primarily for professional development purposes and therefore certain topics are under-represented compared to the original publication, notably resources concerned with communication, education and mental health. The 1993 search identified a gradual increase in resources related to mental illness. These tended to fall into two categories – those that inform about services, and those that question the differential rates of mental illness and varying quality of treatment for people from black and minority ethnic groups.

In terms of priority health issues, as identified in the previous and current national strategies for health (such as CHD and strokes, cancers, mental illness and accidents) and in

*Ethnicity and Health*[2] (diabetes, infant health, haemoglobinopathies and access to health services), the picture is variable.

The 1993 search did not identify any resources specifically on hypertension or strokes, although a few resources included information about CHD in relation to other issues, for example nutrition and physical activity. Since then, a few resources have been produced that address hypertension and strokes.

The resources dealing with cancer have increased fourfold since the original publication. All are aimed at women and are concerned with breast and cervical cancer, although the issue of lung cancer is raised in some of the smoking resources, the majority of which are targeted at men.

Accident prevention is an area that has seen limited growth particularly in relation to children, safety in the home and on the roads. These almost exclusively target communities from the Indian sub-continent.

In relation to sexual health, a large number of resources on HIV/AIDS was identified in 1993, confirming the trend noted in Bhatt and Dickinson's (1992) work[14]. The number of new resources exclusively about contraception declined, possibly because contraception in terms of safer sex and condom use is now often discussed in the context of HIV/AIDS education. Since 1994, the overall number of resources on sexual health, including HIV/AIDS, has declined.

In 1993, antenatal and postnatal care still featured significantly with newer resources developed for communities not previously catered for, such as the Chinese. Some of these dealt with new topics such as the benefits of breastfeeding or information about home birth choices. There are fewer antenatal and postnatal resources in this revised edition, and half of these were included in the original publication.

Although diabetes is four to five times more prevalent in South Asian communities than in non-South Asian communities and twice as prevalent in African–Caribbean communities as in white communities, this is not reflected in the number of resources available. The 1993 search revealed an increase in the number of resources about diabetes but these were almost exclusively aimed at South Asian communities in terms of dietary advice based on a traditional diet. Since then, two new resources have become available for African–Caribbean people, with the remainder aimed at people from the Indian sub-continent.

There is still a lack of resources about haemoglobinopathies, and given the significance of these conditions this is a noticeable gap. The 1993 search found that resources were almost entirely produced by voluntary groups and most were aimed at informing the general population about the existence of sickle cell and thalassaemia, although a few were targeted at children who have the condition to help them understand the illness and treatment. The three resources included in this publication are aimed mainly at health professionals but can be used by people with these conditions.

Resources about nutrition and healthy eating remain popular, although since 1993 the production of audio-cassettes has been a notable development. The majority of the cassettes, however, originate from the same producer, a hospital dietetic and nutrition department, and give advice on specific diets. The nutrition resources are primarily aimed at people from the Indian sub-continent, although there are a few resources for other communities, including the Arabic, Chinese and African–Caribbean communities.

In 1993–94, there were few resources that dealt with alcohol, smoking, drugs and solvent misuse. Since then, the number of smoking resources has trebled from two to six whilst the number of resources about alcohol has remained the same. In the first edition there was one resource about solvents for retailers. This edition includes a booklet on drugs and alcohol for the Somali community and a video for young men that addresses a range of issues including drugs.

# Formats of resources and the development process

Over the past 10 years the quantity and range of health-related resources for black and minority ethnic groups has increased. The choice of formats and the developmental process has also changed (Table 3), reflecting an increase in the level of expertise and experience available.

*Table 3. Number of resources by format*

| Format | Number |
| --- | --- |
| Audio-cassette | 12 |
| Book/let | 25 |
| Multi-media | 1 |
| Pack | 27 |
| Video and video pack | 37 |
| Total | 102 |

The most noticeable development is the increased use of video as a medium for conveying health information. It is a way of taking a message directly into the home and there are indications that some communities prefer health promotion information in this format. It is also an accessible medium irrespective of the literacy level of the audience. Video is often used when the information given is in a language other than English.

Videos have been designed for use in waiting areas, to support routine consultations with health professionals and for direct use in the home. Many videos use drama to open up a topic for discussion, particularly if it is a potentially sensitive issue such as HIV/AIDS.

One of the problems with video as a medium is that it can date quickly. People are used to sophisticated imagery on screen, and changes in fashion can be very noticeable. Equally, if information or advice changes, then the video becomes obsolete unless the facilitator provides supplementary information.

Translation is an important part of the development process when producing information and resources in other languages. Resources produced in the late 1980s and early 1990s, including video/film scripts, were often written in English and then translated into the chosen language or languages. In the case of videos, the script was then dubbed. This frequently resulted in stilted, sometimes clumsy or overly academic scripts, with inappropriate visual representations. As producers became more experienced, text and scripts were developed and written in the chosen language rather than translated from English. Videos designed for different audiences were produced and filmed separately, each with their own script and actors so that the dialogue and people were authentic for that particular language and cultural group.

A positive development in the production of health-related resources is the early involvement of the target communities. This enables health educators and minority ethnic groups to discuss health priorities and needs, and to develop appropriate and therefore effective resources. Many of the more recent videos are of broadcast quality.

This database project confirms that more resources are now available for black and minority ethnic groups and these address a broader range of health issues and concerns, often as a result of the active involvement of the communities themselves.

Lessons are being learnt about consultation with and involvement of black and minority ethnic groups in the development and dissemination of health resources, and producers have become more skilled in resource production. In 1997, the HEA researched and produced some guidance on the development and translation of health information. *Many voices, one message*, reviewed on page 82, reviews what is known about linguistic needs in the UK, presents the case for developing a translation policy and explores the issues involved in translation.

# The resources

At the time of going to press, all the resources included in this publication or on the database were nationally available for purchase or hire. Inclusion of a resource in this publication or on the black and minority ethnic group health-related resources database however, does not imply HEA recommendation.

Each review provides a snapshot of the resource in order to help users identify and select resources appropriate for their purposes. The review is not an evaluation but a description of the resource. It describes:

- who the resource is for;
- who produced it;
- what it covers;
- how information is conveyed;
- any additional information required or omissions;
- how the resource can be used;
- the involvement of target communities in its development and/or testing;
- the accuracy and acceptability of language translations was not evaluated.

It is important to preview a resource yourself before using it in order to ensure that you are familiar with the issues it raises and that you have any additional information required. If you are working with linkworkers and interpreters it will be helpful to ensure that they are also familiar with the resource.

It is not always necessary to purchase resources as they may be held by your local health promotion agency and available for loan. Some items can be obtained from the distributor and previewed for a small charge.

# References

1  Department of Health (1992) *On the state of the public health for 1991: Chief Medical Officer's report*. London: HMSO.

2  Department of Health (1993) *Ethnicity and health – a guide for the NHS*. London: HMSO.

3  Department of Health (1992) *The Health of the Nation*. London: HMSO.

4  Department of Health (1996) *Variations in Health. What can the Department of Health and the NHS do?* London: Department of Health.

5  Rudat K. (1995) *Black and minority ethnic groups in England: health and lifestyles*. London: HEA.

6  Johnson M.R.D., Owen D. and Blackburn C. (1999) *Black and minority ethnic groups in England: the second health and lifestyles survey*. London: HEA.

7  Gervais R.M.C., Jovchelovitch S. (1998) *The health beliefs of the Chinese community in England: a qualitative research study*. London: HEA.

8  *Our Healthier Nation: a contract for health. A consultation paper* (1998). London: The Stationery Office.

9  Department of Health press release, 1.3 million funding for pilot projects to improve ethnic minority health (5 February 1998).

10 *Independent Inquiry into Inequalities in Health Report* (1998). London: The Stationery Office.

11 Department of Health press release, Frank Dobson gives the go-ahead for first wave of health action zones (31 March 1998).

12 Department of Health press release, Fifteen new health action zones to tackle health inequalities (11 August 1998).

13 Bhopal R.S. and Donaldson L.J. (1988) 'Health Education for ethnic minorities – current provision and future directions'. *Health Education Journal* 47, 137–140.

14 Bhatt A. and Dickinson R. (1992) 'An analysis of health education materials for minority communities by cultural and linguistic groups'. *Health Education Journal* 51(2), 72–7.

# How to use this book

The resources in this book are listed alphabetically by title ignoring definite and indefinite articles such as 'The' and 'A'.

Entries for each resource include information about the format, language, target audience, the cost, the producer and date of production and the distributor's name. The address and telephone number of each distributor are also provided. Details such as price change over time, and items may be withdrawn or become out of print, so it is advisable to check the information with the distributor. Please note that the 'Booklet' format refers to books *and* booklets.

## Indexes

Resources are listed under two indexes – a topics index and a languages/communities index.

## Topics index

The resources are indexed by topic, some under more than one. These represent broad categories. The topics index has been amended since the first edition in 1994. Health-related resources for black and minority ethnic groups was the first of the population database series and the topic headings were based on the resources identified in 1993. Since then, the HPiC has developed several more databases for different population groups and it became necessary to standardise the topic headings and bring the index into line with the Health Promotion Thesaurus terms used in HPiC.

## Languages/communities index

This index was based upon the producers' and distributors' descriptions. It lists all those resources produced in languages other than English and those resources targeted at specific communities. There are a number of resources in English that are aimed generally at a range of black and minority ethnic groups, not always specified, and these are not included in this index.

# Appendices

1. Reviewers and critical readers.
2. Directories of black and minority ethnic initiatives and resources.

# Sources of further information

New resources and information appear all the time so it is important to keep up to date with developments. The following organisations can help you do this. A list of key documents is also provided.

## Health Promotion Information Centre (HPiC)

The HPiC at the HEA is the national centre for health promotion information and advice. It offers a range of services to professionals with an interest in health promotion including access the HealthProm*is*, the national database for health promotion which is regularly updated. This database includes documents such as research reports, key papers, journal articles, specialist books, multimedia resources and a series of resource databases, with links to other websites and database.

The reviews included in this book can also be accessed directly on the web at: http://healthpromis.hea.org.uk or via the HPiC pages of the HEA's website at: http://www.hea.org.uk/hpic. You can conduct your own search and check the latest additions to the database, following the guidance provided on the website. A search of the database can also be requested by contacting HpiC via:

Tel: 020 7413 1995; Fax: 020 7413 2605; e-mail: hpic.enquiry@hea.org.uk.

Links to relevant websites can be found at: http://www.hea.org.uk/hpic.

## Local health promotion units/agencies

Local health promotion units and agencies are a valuable source of information and support. Many have reference libraries and resources available for loan, and some may supply leaflets and posters. Specialist health promotion staff may be available to advise on health promotion strategies, issues and topics, and provide training. They will also have details about local initiatives. The address and phone number of your local unit or agency can be found in the telephone directory under your local health authority.

# King's Fund Library

King's Fund Libary
11–13 Cavendish Square
London W1M 0AN
Tel: 020 7307 2568/9
Fax: 020 7307 2805
e-mail: library@kehf.org.uk
web: http://www.kingsfund.org.uk

The library and information service at the King's Fund is a valuable resource for all those involved in the development and management of health and social care services. At present the library is open to the public for reference purposes, but it is possible that a membership scheme will be introduced in 1999.

The King's Fund Share project was disbanded in 1997. However, the library continues to house a substantial collection on black and minority ethnic health. Services on offer include literature searches and the provision of details about relevant published material from the library database. Library staff and a specialist librarian working on ethnic health issues are available to assist with enquiries.

# Ethnic Minorities Health – Current awareness bulletin

The aim of the *Current awareness bulletin* is to index information relating to all aspects of the health of minority groups. Most items listed are journal articles but conference proceedings, theses, books and other items such as audio-visual resources may also be included. The main emphasis relates to British practice but some international references are included if relevant. The quarterly bulletin is available on subscription.

*Ethnic Minorities Health – Current awareness bulletin*
Medical Library
Field House Teaching Centre
Bradford Royal Infirmary
Bradford
West Yorkshire BD9 6RJ
Tel: 01274 364130

# Key documents

The following documents and reports are of national relevance. They draw attention to the health needs of black and minority ethnic groups and have implications for needs assessment, and service development and provision. They will be of interest to commissioners, purchasers and providers of all health care services.

*Beyond the boundary.* NHS Ethnic Health Unit. Leeds: NHS EHU, 1996.

*Coronary heart disease in South Asian communities: a manual for health promotion.* London: HEA, 1994.

*Ethnic health bibliography.* G. Karmi and P. McKeigue. North East, North West Thames Regional Health Authority, 1993.

*Ethnicity and health – a guide for the NHS.* London: Department of Health, 1993.

*Ethnicity and health: Reviews of literature and guidance for purchasers in the areas of cardiovascular disease, mental health and haemoglobinopathies.* CRD Report 5. York: The University of York NHS Centre for Reviews and Dissemination Social Policy Research Unit, 1996.

*Equality across the board: report of a working party on black and ethnic minority non-executive members.* NAHAT and King's Fund, 1993.

*Update on equality across the board.* NAHAT and King's Fund. Birmingham: NAHAT, 1996.

*Facing up to the difference.* Department of Health and the King's Fund, 1996.

*Good practice and quality indicators in primary healthcare.* Leeds: NHS Ethnic Health Unit, 1996.

*Guidelines for the implementation of ethnic monitoring in health service provision: a complete guide for setting up ethnic monitoring.* North East, North West Thames Regional Health Authority, 1992.

*Black and minority ethnic groups in England: health and lifestyles.* London: HEA, 1995.

*The health beliefs of the Chinese community in England: a qualitative research study.* London: HEA, 1998.

*Health for all our children: achieving appropriate health care for black and minority ethnic children and their families.* London: Action for Sick Children, 1993.

*Infant feeding in Asian families.* London: ONS, 1997.

*On the state of the public health for 1991: Chief Medical Officer's report.* (Includes a chapter, 'Health of black and ethnic minorities'.) London: HMSO, 1992.

*Physical activity 'from our point of view': qualitative research among South Asian and black communities.* London: HEA, 1997.

*Primary health care for black and minority ethnic people: a GP perspective.* London: NHS Ethnic Health Unit, 1996.

*Responding to diversity: a study of commissioning issues and good practice in purchasing minority ethnic health.* London: OPM, 1996.

*Safety and minority ethnic communities: a report on the home safety information needs of Asian, Chinese and Vietnamese communities.* Birmingham: Royal Society for the Prevention of Accidents, 1993.

*Sickle cell and thalassaemia: achieving health gain. Guidance for commissioners and providers.* London: HEA, 1998.

*Sickle cell, thalassaemia and other haemoglobinopathies. Report of a working party of the Standing Medical Advisory Committee on sickle cell, thalassaemia and other haemoglobinopathies.* London: HMSO, 1993.

# Topics index

## Access to health services

### Book/let
Call for care
Current treatments for HIV: a guide for
African communities in the UK

### Pack
Caring for patients. A multi-cultural
illustrated guide
Essential Urdu and Hindi for hospitals and
general practice
Health check-up photo-pack
The NHS home healthcare guide
Our healthier nation: a contract for health.
A summary of the consultation document

### Video
Advocates can help you
Black and ethnic minority clients:
meeting needs
Good health in later life: a guide to health
and social services for Bengali elders

## Access to community services

### Book/let
Call for care

### Video
Advocates can help you
Good health in later life: a guide to health
and social services for Bengali elders

## Advocacy

### Video
Black and ethnic minority clients:
meeting needs
Advocates can help you

## Alcohol

### Booklet
Drugs and alcohol. A guide for Somalis
Your drink and you

### Pack
Alcohol misuse and Asian communities:
a health awareness pack
Four by four

### Video
Big night out
Safe: a video resource for work with
young men

# Ante/postnatal care

## Audio-cassette
Ante-natal care for you and your baby
Talking about miscarriage

## Book/let
Baby matters. HIV, pregnancy and
childbearing issues for African women
Maternity services for Asian women
While you are pregnant: how to avoid
infection from food and contact
with animals

## Video
Pregnancy and childbirth

# Child health

## Video
Child safety in the home
Immunisation: a guide for parents
Play and child development
Safely home?

# Communication
(includes language development,
translation, interpreting, ESOL materials
and specific communication disorders)

## Book/let
Caring for patients. A multi-cultural
illustrated guide
Many voices, one message. Guidance for
the development and translation of health
information

## Pack
The body map

Essential Urdu and Hindi for hospitals and
general practice
Health check-up photo-pack
Reaching people: guidelines for the
development and evaluation of sexual
health materials in a multi-racial society

## Video
Black and ethnic minority clients:
meeting needs

# Drugs and solvent misuse

## Booklet
Drugs and alcohol: a guide for Somalis

## Video
Safe: a video resource for work with
young men

# Education

## Pack
Partnership with parents: an anti-
discriminatory approach
Religion, ethnicity and sex education:
exploring the issues

## Video
Are we missing out?

# Environment

## Book/let
Keep warm, keep well

# Equal opportunities

## Book/let
Speaking out

## Pack
Challenging racism (CEDC)
Challenging racism (Independence Educational Publishers)
Combating racial prejudice against Irish people
Combating racial prejudice against Jewish people
Equal opportunities: activities for PSE and general studies in secondary schools
The equalizer 2: activity ideas for empowerment work and anti-racist work with young people
One world. A race and culture activity pack for youth workers
Partnership with parents: an anti-discriminatory approach
Racial equality means business: a standard for racial equality for employers
Young and equal. A standard for racial equality in services working with young people

## Video
Are we missing out?
Travelling people

# Health conditions and illnesses

## Cancer

### Booklet
Calling all women: health checks that can save your life

### Pack
Breast screening training pack for minority women

Woman to woman: cervical screening training pack for minority women

### Video
Health in your hands. A guide to cervical screening
A picture of health: breast screening

# Cardiovascular disease
## Audio-cassette
Take care of your heart

## Book/let
High blood pressure, hypertension, pressure
Hypertension and the African-Caribbean community. Guidance for health professionals
Stroke: questions and answers

## Pack
Asian language CHD patient pack

# Continence
## Video
Promoting continence for women

# Cystic fibrosis
## Audio-cassette
Cystic fibrosis: diagnosis and adolescence

# Diabetes
## Audio-cassette
Healthy eating for people with diabetes

## Book/let
Diabetes: a guide for African–Caribbean people
Diabetes: a guide for South Asian people
Healthy Asian cooking: a guide for people from the Indian sub-continent

## Video

Damage caused to the body by diabetes
Diabetes: a guide for African–Caribbean people
Driving with diabetes and Travel and diabetes
Hypoglycaemia and coping with diabetes during illness

# Sickle cell

## Booklet

Sickle cell anaemia

## Pack

Sickle cell anaemia and thalassaemia teaching pack

# Thalassaemia

## Pack

Sickle cell anaemia and thalassaemia teaching pack
What is thalassaemia?

# Immunisation

## Video

Immunisation: a guide for parents

# Infant feeding

## Audio-cassette

Weaning your baby or Ababinta Ilmahaaga

## Video

A healthy balance: a guide for parents in four languages
Starting your baby on solid foods
Weaning

# Mental health

## Pack

Schizophrenia: notes for relatives and friends and Psychiatric diagnosis: notes for relatives and patients

## Video

Safe: a video resource for work with young men

# Nutrition

## Audio-cassette

Advice for a low phosphate diet
Advice for a low potassium diet
Advice for a low potassium and low phosphate diet
Advice for lowering salt and fluid intake
Healthy eating for people with diabetes
Healthy eating for people who have high fat levels
Healthy eating for people who wish to lose weight
Take care of your heart

## Book/let

Food and culture
Healthy Asian cooking. A guide for people from the Indian sub-continent
Healthy eating the Moroccan way

## Multimedia

World of food

## Video

Eating well: feeling good
Enjoying our healthy food
A healthy balance: a guide for parents in four languages
Healthy meals in Britain today: Bengali recipes

Healthy meals in Britain today:
Caribbean recipes
Healthy meals in Britain today:
Chinese recipes

# Older people

## Video
Good health in later life: a guide to health
and social services for Bengali elders

# Oral health

## Pack
Chinese oral health education materials

## Video
A beautiful smile
Teeth for life

# Parenting

## Pack
Caring for other people's children: a guide
for private foster carers

## Video
Play and child development

# Physical activity

## Audio-cassette
Take care of your heart

## Video
Keep active, keep healthy

# Professional education and development

## Pack
Partnership with parents: an anti-
discriminatory approach

## Video
Black and ethnic minority clients:
meeting needs

# Religion

## Journal
World religions in education 1997/98 –
Who am 1? The search for individual
and group identity

## Pack
Religion, ethnicity and sex education:
exploring the issues

# Safety

## Video
Child safety in the home
Safely home?

# Screening

## Pack
Breast screening training pack for minority
women
Health check-up photo-pack
Woman to woman: cervical screening
training pack for minority women

## Video
Health in your hands. A guide to
cervical screening
A picture of health: breast screening

# Sexual health and personal relationships

## Book/let
Baby matters. HIV, pregnancy and
childbearing issues for African women
Current treatments for HIV: a guide for
African communities in the UK
Meet Fatima, a girl who has HIV
Men's matters: a guide for African men
on HIV and AIDS
Reaching people – guidelines for the
development and evaluation of sexual
health materials in a multiracial society
Religion, ethnicity and sex education:
exploring the issues
Women's matters: an introduction to HIV
for African women

## Pack
Religion, ethnicity and sex education:
exploring the issues
Rishtae aur zimmevarian: relationships and
responsibilities: sexual health programme
with black and minority ethnic
communities. A training pack and report

## Video
Boys on the game
Oceans apart – an interactive drama and
video project on HIV for women
Safe: a video resource for work with
young men

# Smoking

## Audio-cassette
Take care of your heart

## Video
A beautiful smile
The cost of smoking
Give up smoking for the good life
A new life. A health education drama
about smoking
The smoke inside us

# Travellers

## Video
Are we missing out?
Travelling people

# Women's health

## Audio-cassette
Talking about miscarriage

## Book/let
Baby matters. HIV, pregnancy and
childbearing issues for African women
Calling all women: health checks that can
save your life
Maternity services for Asian women
Speaking out
While you are pregnant: how to avoid
infection from food and contact
with animals

## Pack
Breast screening training pack for minority
women
Health check-up photo-pack

Woman to woman: cervical screening
training pack for minority women

## Video
Health in your hands. A guide to cervical
screening
Keep active, keep healthy
Oceans apart – an interactive drama and
video project on HIV for women
A picture of health: breast screening
Promoting continence for women

# Work and the workplace

## Pack
Racial equality means business: a standard
for racial equality for employers

# Languages/communities index

## African

### Book/let
Baby matters. HIV, pregnancy and childbearing issues for African women
Current treatments for HIV: a guide for African communities in the UK
Meet Fatima, a girl who has HIV
Men's matters: a guide for African men on HIV and AIDS
Speaking out
Women's matters: an introduction to HIV for African women

### Video
Oceans apart – an interactive drama and video project on HIV/AIDS for women
A picture of health: breast screening
Safe: a video resource for work with young men

## African–Caribbean (English language)

### Book/let
Diabetes: a guide for African–Caribbean people
High blood pressure, hypertension, pressure
Hypertension and the African–Caribbean community. Guidance for health professionals
Speaking out
Your drink and you

### Pack
Breast screening training pack for minority women
Woman to woman: cervical screening training pack for minority women

### Video
Boys on the game
Diabetes: a guide for African–Caribbean people
Healthy meals in Britain today: Caribbean recipes
Oceans apart – an interactive drama and video project on HIV/AIDS for women
A picture of health: breast screening
Safe: a video resource for work with young men

# Arabic

## Book/let
Caring for patients. A multi-cultural
illustrated guide
Healthy eating the Moroccan way
Our Healthier Nation: a contract
for health. A summary of the
consultation paper

## Pack
The body map
Woman to woman: cervical screening
training pack for minority women

## Video
Advocates can help you
Health in your hands. A guide to
cervical screening

# Bengali (including Sylheti speakers)

## Audio-cassette
Ante-natal care for you and your baby
Take care of your heart (Sylheti)
Talking about miscarriage (Sylheti)

## Book/let
Calling all women: health checks that
can save your life
Caring for patients. A multi-cultural
illustrated guide
Diabetes: a guide for South Asian people
Healthy Asian cooking: a guide for people
from the Indian sub-continent
Keep warm, keep well
The NHS home healthcare guide
Our Healthier Nation: a contract
for health. A summary of the
consultation paper
Stroke: questions and answers

While you are pregnant: how to avoid
infection from food and from contact
with animals

## Pack
Asian language CHD patient pack
The body map
Breast screening training pack for
minority women
Four by four
Health check-up photo-pack
Schizophrenia: notes for relatives
and friends
Woman to woman: cervical screening
training pack for minority women

## Video
Advocates can help you
A beautiful smile
Child safety in the home
The cost of smoking
Damage caused to the body by diabetes
Driving with diabetes and Travel
and diabetes
Enjoying our healthy food (Sylheti)
Good health in later life: a guide to health
and social services for Bengali elders
Health in your hands. A guide to cervical
screening (Sylheti)
Healthy meals in Britain today:
Bengali recipes
Hypoglycaemia and coping with diabetes
during illness
Keep active, keep healthy
New life. A health education drama about
smoking (Sylheti)
Play and child development (and Sylheti)
Promoting continence for women
Safely home?
Starting your baby on solid foods
Teeth for life
Weaning

# Chinese (Cantonese speaking)

## Audio-cassette
Ante-natal care for you and your baby

## Book/let
Calling all women: health checks that can save your life
Caring for patients. A multi-cultural illustrated guide
Keep warm, keep well
The NHS home healthcare guide

Our Healthier Nation: a contract for health. A summary of the consultation paper
Stroke: questions and answers
While you are pregnant: how to avoid infection from food and from contact with animals

## Pack
Breast screening training pack for minority women
Chinese oral health education materials
Woman to woman: cervical screening training pack for minority women

## Video
Advocates can help you
A healthy balance: a guide for parents in four languages
Healthy meals in Britain today: Chinese recipes

# Farsi

## Pack
The body map

# French

## Book/let
Caring for patients. A multi-cultural illustrated guide
Current treatments for HIV: a guide for African communities in the UK

## Pack
The body map

# German

## Book/let
Caring for patients. A multi-cultural illustrated guide

# Greek

## Book/let
Caring for patients. A multi-cultural illustrated guide
Keep warm, keep well
Our Healthier Nation: a contract for health. A summary of the consultation paper
While you are pregnant: how to avoid infection from food and from contact with animals

# Gujarati

## Audio-cassette
Advice for a low phosphate diet
Advice for a low potassium diet
Advice for a low potassium and low phosphate diet
Advice for lowering salt and fluid intake

Ante-natal care for you and your baby
Cystic fibrosis: diagnosis and adolescence
Healthy eating for people with diabetes
Healthy eating for people who have high fat levels
Healthy eating for people who wish to lose weight

## Book/let
Call for care
Calling all women: health checks that can save your life
Caring for patients. A multi-cultural illustrated guide
Diabetes: a guide for South Asian people
Healthy Asian cooking: a guide for people from the Indian sub-continent
Keep warm, keep well
The NHS home healthcare guide
Stroke: questions and answers
While you are pregnant: how to avoid infection from food and from contact with animals

## Pack
Asian language CHD patient pack
The body map
Breast screening training pack for minority women
Four by four
Health check-up photo-pack

## Video
Advocates can help you
A beautiful smile
A healthy balance: a guide for parents in four languages
Immunisation: a guide for parents
Keep active, keep healthy
Play and child development
Weaning

# Hindi

## Audio-cassette
Advice for a low phosphate diet
Advice for a low potassium diet
Advice for a low potassium and low phosphate diet
Advice for lowering salt and fluid intake
Ante-natal care for you and your baby
Healthy eating for people with diabetes
Healthy eating for people who have high fat levels
Healthy eating for people who wish to lose weight

## Book/let
Calling all women: health checks that can save your life
Caring for patients. A multi-cultural illustrated guide
Diabetes: a guide for South Asian people
Healthy Asian cooking: a guide for people from the Indian sub-continent
Keep warm, keep well
The NHS home healthcare guide
Our Healthier Nation: a contract for health. A summary of the consultation paper
Stroke: questions and answers
While you are pregnant: how to avoid infection from food and from contact with animals

## Pack
Asian language CHD patient pack
Breast screening training pack for minority women
Essential Urdu/Hindi for hospitals and general practice
Health check-up photo-pack

## Video
A beautiful smile
Immunisation: a guide for parents
Keep active, keep healthy

Play and child development
Weaning

# Italian

## Book/let
Caring for patients. A multi-cultural illustrated guide

# Mirpuri/Urdu

## Audio-cassette
Talking about miscarriage

## Pack
Woman to woman: cervical screening training pack for minority women

# Polish

## Book/let
Caring for patients. A multi-cultural illustrated guide
Keep warm, keep well

# Punjabi

## Audio-cassette
Advice for a low phosphate diet
Advice for a low potassium diet
Advice for a low potassium and low phosphate diet
Advice for lowering salt and fluid intake
Ante-natal care for you and your baby
Healthy eating for people with diabetes
Healthy eating for people who have high fat levels

Healthy eating for people who wish to lose weight

## Book/let
Call for care
Calling all women: health checks that can save your life
Caring for patients. A multi-cultural illustrated guide
Diabetes: a guide for South Asian people
Healthy Asian cooking: a guide for people from the Indian sub-continent
Keep warm, keep well
The NHS home healthcare guide
Our Healthier Nation: a contract for health. A summary of the consultation paper
Stroke: questions and answers
While you are pregnant: how to avoid infection from food and from contact with animals

## Pack
Asian language CHD patient pack
The body map
Breast screening training pack for minority women
Four by four
Health check-up photo-pack
Schizophrenia: notes for relatives and friends

## Video
Advocates can help you
A healthy balance: a guide for parents in four languages
Immunistaion: a guide for parents
Keep active, keep healthy
Promoting continence for women
Teeth for life
Weaning

## Pushto

### Video
Enjoying our healthy food

## Somali

### Audio-cassette
Weaning your baby or Ababinta Ilmahaaga

### Book/let
Calling all women: health checks that
can save your life
Drugs and alcohol: a guide for somalis
or Maandooriyayaasha Iyo Khamriga:
wargelin – af Soomaali
Our Healthier Nation: a contract
for health. A summary of the
consultation paper

### Pack
The body map

### Video
Advocates can help you
Child safety in the home
The cost of smoking
Eating well: feeling good
Health in your hands. A guide to
cervical screening

## Spanish

### Book/let
Caring for patients. A multi-cultural
illustrated guide

## Tamil

### Pack
The body map

## Turkish

### Book/let
Calling all women: health checks that
can save your life
Caring for patients. A multi-cultural
illustrated guide
Keep warm, keep well
Our Healthier Nation: a contract
for health. A summary of the
consultation paper
While you are pregnant: how to avoid
infection from food and from contact
with animals

### Video
Advocates can help you
Child safety in the home
Give up smoking for the good life
Health in your hands. A guide to
cervical screening
The smoke inside us

## Urdu

### Audio-cassette
Advice for a low phosphate diet
Advice for a low potassium diet
Advice for a low potassium and low
phosphate diet
Advice for lowering salt and fluid intake
Ante-natal care for you and your baby
Cystic fibrosis: diagnosis and adolescence
Healthy eating for people with diabetes
Healthy eating for people who have high
fat levels

Healthy eating for people who wish to
lose weight
Talking about miscarriage

# Book/let
Call for care
Calling all women: health checks that
can save your life
Caring for patients. A multi-cultural
illustrated guide
Diabetes: a guide for South Asian people
Healthy Asian cooking: a guide for people
from the Indian sub-continent
Keep warm, keep well
The NHS home healthcare guide
Our Healthier Nation: a contract
for health. A summary of the
consultation paper
Stroke: questions and answers
While you are pregnant: how to avoid
infection from food and from contact
with animals

# Pack
The body map
Breast screening training pack for
minority women
Essential Urdu/Hindi for hospitals
and general practice
Four by four
Health check-up photo-pack
Schizophrenia: notes for relatives
and friends

# Video
A beautiful smile
Child safety in the home
Enjoying our healthy food
Play and child development
Promoting continence for women
Safely home?
Teeth for life
Weaning

# Vietnamese

## Book/let
Calling all women: health checks that
can save your life
The NHS home healthcare guide
Our Healthier Nation: a contract
for health. A summary of the
consultation paper

## Pack
Breast screening training pack for
minority women
Woman to woman: cervical screening
training pack for minority women

# Welsh

## Book/let
Keep warm, keep well

# Yemeni

## Audio-cassette
Ante-natal care for you and your baby

# Resources

# Ababinta Ilmahaaga

*See* Weaning your baby

# Advice for a low phosphate diet

**FORMAT** Audio-cassette, untimed; advice sheet A4, 2-pages English; advice sheet A4, 2-pages Gujarati, Hindi, Punjabi and Urdu
**LANGUAGE(S)** English, Gujarati, Hindi, Punjabi and Urdu
**AUDIENCE** General public, primary health care team
**PRICE** £2.50+p&p (English cassette); £3.00+p&p (other language versions); £1.00+p&p (advice sheets)
**PRODUCER** London: Nutrition and Dietetic Department, Hammersmith Hospital,1995
**DISTRIBUTOR** Nutrition and Dietetic Department, Hammersmith Hospital, Du Cane Road, London W12 0HS. Tel: 020 8743 2030; Fax: 020 8740 3169

These cassettes provide information for people needing to follow a low phosphate diet. They explain the food choices that can be made to help control phosphate intake for people whose kidneys do not work properly. The cassettes were produced by the dietitians at Hammersmith Hospital and are available in five languages.

The cassettes use a question and answer format to explain phosphate, phosphate and kidney problems, management of its intake through selective dieting and taking phosphate binder tables. Recommended foods and those containing high and low amounts of phosphate are listed.

Readers may want to clarify advice on eating up to seven eggs per week against concerns about cholesterol, and consuming fizzy drinks given their high sugar content.

Information is reassuring, brief and practical. The accompanying transcript, presented as a leaflet and written in a formal style may be off-putting if the news of the condition is upsetting. Practice nurses may need to offer counselling, establish that users have access to a cassette and that leaflet print size is appropriate.

Useful as a self-help or group work resource for people recently diagnosed as needing to follow a low phosphate diet. Primary care workers, carers and family members would find this informative.

# Advice for a low potassium diet

**FORMAT** Audio-cassette, untimed; Notes A4, 3-pages English; advice sheet A4, 2-pages Hindi, Gujarati, Punjabi and Urdu
**LANGUAGE** English, Gujarati, Hindi, Punjabi and Urdu
**AUDIENCE** General public, primary health care team
**PRICE** £2.50+p&p (English cassette); £3.00+p&p (translated cassette); £1.00+p&p (advice sheets)
**PRODUCER** London: Nutrition and Dietetic Department, Hammersmith Hospital,1995
**DISTRIBUTOR** Nutrition and Dietetic Department, Hammersmith Hospital, Du Cane Road, London W12 0HS. Tel: 020 8743 2030; Fax: 020 8740 3169

This resource is a three-page information sheet that has also been transcribed on to a short audio-cassette. The resource is aimed at English patients and patients from the Indian sub-continent who have been prescribed a low potassium diet for health reasons relating to kidney functioning. Produced by dietitians at Hammersmith Hospital, London, the resource aims to give patients information about how to follow a low potassium diet.

The information, in question and answer format covers the following issues: 'What is potassium?', 'Why has potassium become a problem now that your kidneys are no longer working properly?', 'Is there anything you can do about this?', 'Which foods are high in potassium?', 'What about cooking vegetables?', 'What other foods should you avoid?', 'What about drinks?', 'What foods and drinks can you have?' and 'Other foods which are also allowed'. It also suggests that a patient's dietitian can provide further information and advice relevant to an individual's particular circumstances.

The sorts of food that are mentioned include English and South Asian meals, snacks and low cost foods. The resource could be used by patients in their own homes after specialist advice and treatment.

The tape would be a useful source of information for adults who cannot read or who have a visual impairment.

# Advice for a low potassium and low phosphate diet

**FORMAT** Audio-cassette, untimed; advice sheet A4, 3-pages English; Advice sheet A4, 3-pages Gujarati, Hindi, Punjabi and Urdu
**LANGUAGE** English, Gujarati, Hindi, Punjabi and Urdu
**AUDIENCE** General public, primary health care team
**PRICE** £2.50+p&p (English cassette); £3.00+p&p (other language versions); £1.00+p&p (advice sheets)
**PRODUCER** London: Nutrition and Dietetic Department, Hammersmith Hospital,1995
**DISTRIBUTOR** Nutrition and Dietetic Department, Hammersmith Hospital, Du Cane Road, London W12 0HS. Tel: 020 8743 2030; Fax: 020 8740 3169

These cassettes aim to provide a basic practical healthy eating guide for people who need to follow a low potassium and low phosphate diet. They were produced by the dietitians at Hammersmith Hospital and are available in five languages.

Using a question and answer format the audio cassette explains potassium and phosphate, why high levels are a concern, the effects on the body of rising levels of potassium and its control through careful attention to diet and tablets. Potassium levels in various foods are given, and recommended foods and those to avoid are listed with cooking tips, for example boiling vegetables in lots of water.

Information is reassuring, brief and practical. The accompanying transcript, presented as a leaflet and written in a formal style, may be off-putting if the news of this condition is upsetting. Practice nurses may need to offer counselling, establish that users have access to a cassette and that the leaflet print size is appropriate.

Useful as a self-help or group work resource for people recently diagnosed as needing to follow a low potassium and low phosphate diet. Primary health care workers, carers and family members would find this informative.

# Advice for lowering salt and fluid intake

**FORMAT** Audio-cassette, untimed; advice sheet A4, 3-pages English; advice sheet A4, 3-pages Gujarati, Hindi, Punjabi and Urdu
**LANGUAGE** English, Gujarati, Hindi, Punjabi and Urdu
**AUDIENCE** General public, primary health care team

**PRICE** £2.50+p&p (English cassette);
£3.00+p&p (other language versions);
£1.00+p&p (advice sheets)
**PRODUCER** London: Nutrition and
Dietetic Department, Hammersmith
Hospital,1995
**DISTRIBUTOR** Nutrition and Dietetic
Department, Hammersmith Hospital,
Du Cane Road, London W12 0HS.
Tel: 020 8743 2030; Fax: 020 8740 3169

These cassettes aim to provide a basic
practical healthy eating guide for people
who need to reduce their salt and fluid
intake. They are intended for people newly
diagnosed with kidney problems for use
as a self-help resource. The cassettes
were produced by the dietitians at
Hammersmith Hospital and are
available in five languages.

Part one of the audio-cassette explains why
salt intake has become a problem and looks
at: managing salt intake – avoiding salty
snacks, popadoms, cheesy biscuits etc.;
processed foods; reducing salt in cooking;
adding none to cooked food and avoiding
LoSalt which is high in potassium and
should not be used.

Part two covers the reasons for controlling
fluid intake, prevention of fluid build up in
the body and its management, including
careful attention to food and drink
consumed. A summary of self-help tips is
given. The information provided is general
and patients with other problems such as
diabetes will need to seek additional
advice. The tape is a useful way of putting
the information across to those who have
access to an audio-cassette player. The
formally written transcript presented in an
accompanying leaflet may be off-putting if
the news of this condition is upsetting.

# Advocates can help you

**FORMAT** Video, 12 min
**LANGUAGE** English; also available in
Arabic, Bengali, Cantonese, Gujarati,
Punjabi, Somali, Sylheti and Turkish
**AUDIENCE** Black and minority ethnic
groups, health care and community
workers
**PRICE** £15.00+VAT
**PRODUCER** Bromley: Hygia
Communications, 1996
**DISTRIBUTOR** Hygia Communications,
Video Sales Department, PO Box 11,
Bromley BR2 7RW. Tel: 020 8289 9559;
Fax: 020 8462 3206

This video shows how advocates can help
people access health and social services.
It is presented by a black, female health
professional and includes interviews with
people from several ethnic backgrounds
who talk about their personal experiences
of using advocates and the benefits gained.
A health or community worker could use
it as a prompt to enable discussion.

The viewer learns that advocates work
within communities and understand those
particular cultures. Many advocates are
attached to local GP practices/health
centres and will understand not only
the health system but also the work of
the local community including housing,
social services, the education services
and legal services. The video explains
that advocates can help a person who
is nervous, embarrassed, confused or
inhibited, as well as those not able to
speak English.

The video shows a health screening session
in progress and demonstrates the advocacy
process. Some of the problems specific
to refugees are highlighted. The video
presents a wide range of people who

have used advocates to help them with a variety of problems. Examples are: how to use the health centre; miscarriage; pregnancy; hospital appointments; immunisations; housing; not being able to speak any English.

Family members or friends who can speak English may be able to help with translating conversations. However, translators do not provide quite the same service as advocates. In particular, children who are used as translators may not always understand all that is being said, and close friends or relatives may get upset if they think the news given is bad news. There are also confidential and private matters, perhaps about sex or children, that the 'client/patient' may not want to share with a family member/friend.

Regional variations in advocacy services are recognised and advice is given on how to access help and support.

The useful information in this video is summed up by the presenter who tells the viewer that an advocate can be a friend who lends help and support to enable you to get the most out of the health system.

# Alcohol misuse and Asian communities – a health awareness pack

**FORMAT** Pack, 26-pages
**LANGUAGE** English
**AUDIENCE** Health care professionals, health promotion specialists, alcohol advisory agencies
**PRICE** £6.90 inc.
**PRODUCER** London: EACH, 1996
**DISTRIBUTOR** Ethnic Alcohol Counselling in Hounslow, 65–73 Staines Road, Hounslow, London TW3 3HW.
Tel: 020 8577 6059

This pack is for health professionals working with Asian communities. It is published by EACH, a national initiative for the Asian communities on alcohol misuse and health promotion. The pack was funded by the Department of Health. It makes reference to the targets for reducing alcohol consumption levels that were set as part of the previous *Health of the Nation* strategy.

The aim of the pack is to provide a strategic approach to developing health awareness in the Asian communities although the focus is mainly on alcohol and alcohol misuse. Divided into four sections, the pack covers: introduction; background issues; health promotion techniques; and resource materials. The pack provides practical support in working with the Asian communities, for example it examines religious and cultural attitudes, language and women.

The pack looks at different approaches that can be used such as multi-agency intervention work and sessions targeted at particular groups, for example young people. There are also suggestions for monitoring and evaluating work. A list of health awareness publications and materials, some of which are Asian specific, is included.

# Antenatal care for you and your baby

**FORMAT** Audio-cassette, 15 min (copyright free); with leaflets and A2 poster
**LANGUAGE** Cassette available in Bengali, Cantonese, English, Gujarati, Hindi, Punjabi, Urdu, Yemeni. Poster captioned in same languages. Leaflet available in Bengali/English, Cantonese/English, Hindi/English and Urdu/English
**AUDIENCE** Women

**PRICE** Cassette/leaflet/poster £35.00 per language. Various price packages available for multiple copies
**PRODUCER** Birmingham: South Birmingham Health Authority, 1993
**DISTRIBUTOR** Birmingham Women's Hospital, Queen Elizabeth Medical Centre, Edgbaston, Birmingham B15 2TG.
Tel: 0121 472 1377

This resource is targeted at women who do not speak English. It aims to increase awareness and understanding of routine antenatal care, some common screening procedures in pregnancy and the use of foetal movement charts.

A female presenter talks in a friendly and informal manner to the listener. She explains the purpose of antenatal care, outlining what happens at a booking visit and the choices available in antenatal care. Some information (ultrasound, amniocentesis, cardiovascular system, smoking and passive smoking) is described in detail. The cassette states that women will be given a foetal movement 'kick chart'. This is standard procedure in Birmingham but may not be elsewhere, so presenters should check this and advise women accordingly. Mention is made of language barriers and the availability of interpreters and linkworkers but no advice is given on how to arrange these. This will need to be considered when women are given the cassette. Women may also be interested in antenatal classes in their language as the cassette promotes attendance at classes. They will also need information about choices in antenatal care available locally.

Leaflets in some of the languages accompany the cassette and briefly reinforce the main points. The print on the leaflets and the poster is quite small. The poster advertises the cassettes and is designed to encourage women to ask for them. Women who do not speak English will find the cassette encouraging and informative, but it is only an introduction to antenatal care and will need to be supported by health professionals who can communicate with women either directly or through interpreters/linkworkers. The cassette has been piloted in all languages and women were very positive in their response to the resource, valuing the opportunity to have some information in their mother tongue. They were developed by midwives and linkworkers.

# Are we missing out?

**FORMAT** Video, 26 min; leaflet
**LANGUAGE** English
**AUDIENCE** Travellers – parents, teachers of travellers, and traveller education services
**PRICE** Free (single copy)
**PRODUCER** London: Department for Education and Employment, 1998
**DISTRIBUTOR** DfEE, PO Box 5050, Sudbury, Suffolk CO10 6ZQ.
Tel: 020 8602 2260; Fax: 020 8603 3360

This video is aimed at gypsy travellers and is about four young people who are all travellers but regularly attend secondary school. Aimed at parents, this video tries to promote a positive message about education and to encourage parents to support their children's education.

Whilst many travellers are happy to send their children to primary school, some have worries about secondary school. This video recounts the experiences of:
● Clarence (16 years) who likes to ride horses, is a champion boxer and enjoys drawing and pottery. He is good at looking after toddlers.
● John Paul (14 years) who loves football and enjoys schools. His favourite subjects are maths, French, science and PE.

- Esther (18 years) who is at sixth form college studying A-levels. She wants to continue and study for a university degree. She hopes to become a solicitor.
- Sadie (11 years) who likes school and enjoys science, maths and English, especially reading. Her favourite story is 'Stella Luna' by Janell Cannon, because Stella Luna is accepted even though she is different.

The parents of these four children recount their own memories of growing up and intermittent school attendance, most did not go to secondary education. Some were bullied at school while others were intimidated by disinterested teachers. All of them had family responsibilities that prevented them from obtaining a full education. The parents want things to be different for their children. They want their children to have a proper education and be treated properly.

The video shows how the parents support their children's education, financially, academically and with pastoral care. They visit their children's school, liaise with their teachers, and know that the schools respect their culture and their wishes as parents.

The children are happy, articulate individuals, friendly with their peers and have positive self-esteem. The only difference for them, as travellers, is as one of them says, 'We choose to live in a caravan or trailer and they choose to live in a house'.

This video could be used with the parents of travellers, with teachers and schools, to promote a positive approach to the children of travellers and encourage their participation in secondary education.

## Asian language CHD patient pack

**FORMAT** Pack: booklets x 5; A3 colour poster; drug information sheets x 3; fold-out diet sheet
**LANGUAGE** Bengali, English, Gujarati, Hindi and Punjabi
**AUDIENCE** Health care professionals
**PRICE** Free to general practitioners
**PRODUCER** Hoddesdon: Merck Sharp & Dohme Limited, 1995
**DISTRIBUTOR** Freepost, Mother Tongue Campaign, PO Box 5315 London W6 OW2

This information pack is about coronary heart disease (CHD) and its prevention. The target audience is adults from the Indian sub-continent who are at risk of, or who have already suffered from, CHD. The resource can be used by doctors or nurses when giving basic initial information about preventing heart disease or when either of the two drugs mentioned are prescribed.

The pack comprises four information leaflets, a booklet, two copies of a dual language menu card, a poster and two drug information sheets.

The four information leaflets cover 'Answering your questions about cholesterol', 'Why is a cholesterol check important for you now', 'Learning to lower blood pressure' and 'Cholesterol casebook: two case studies'. They present basic facts and tips about how to deal with or prevent health problems relating to heart disease. Information is presented in a question and answer format. For example, questions include: 'What causes excess cholesterol?' 'What sort of foods should one cut down on?' 'How does my doctor know I have hypertension?' 'Will a change in diet lower my blood pressure?'. The case studies describe two personal experiences of diagnosing and treating angina and a heart attack.

The booklet, 'Coronary heart disease: your questions answered', describes the causes and effects and what can be done to reduce the risks. It covers diet, exercise, cholesterol, smoking, stress, blood pressure, diabetes, alcohol intake, being overweight and family history, with half a page to a page of information and advice on each area.

The sample menu card gives a day's suggested food intake as well as a chart that specifies which foods to avoid and which foods can be consumed in greater quantities. The types of food suggested include English and Asian diets.

The poster highlights and warns of the risk factors for heart disease. The pack uses culturally appropriate photographs.

The two information sheets explain about the drugs 'Innovace' and 'Zocor' that are used to treat heart problems and cholesterol. They cover: what is in the tablets, how they work and should be taken, why they need to be taken, side effects and other considerations such as alcohol. This pack was produced by Merck, Sharp & Dohme who manufacture these drugs.

# Baby matters: HIV, pregnancy and childbearing issues for African women

**FORMAT** Booklet, 28-pages, illustrated
**LANGUAGE** English
**AUDIENCE** African women, primary health care teams, professionals working in sexual health and antenatal clinics
**AUTHOR(S)** D. Vowles

**PRICE** Single copies free
**PRODUCER** London: African Community Involvement Association (ACIA) and The Terrence Higgins Trust, 1998
**DISTRIBUTOR** The Terrence Higgins Trust, 52–54 Grays Inn Road, London WC1X 8JU. Tel: 020 7831 0330; Fax: 020 7816 4563; Website: www.tht.org.uk

This booklet is for African women, particularly those who are pregnant or considering pregnancy, and their partners. It aims to inform women, including HIV positive women, about HIV/AIDS and the implications for pregnancy. The emphasis is on personal choice and helping women to obtain the information they want.

Some basic information about HIV/AIDS is provided. The booklet is then divided into two parts covering HIV testing in antenatal clinics, and information for HIV positive women. This is presented as a series of questions and answers.

Part one is aimed at women who are pregnant or thinking about becoming pregnant who have not had a recent test for HIV. It explains why the HIV test is recommended for pregnant women, where this can be done and women's rights regarding HIV testing. The booklet explores the advantages and disadvantages of testing and what women need to think about before they have an HIV test.

Part two is aimed at women who know they are HIV positive and who are either pregnant or thinking about having a baby. This explains how HIV affects pregnancy and how pregnancy affects HIV, including the best time to get pregnant, taking anti-HIV medication and ways to reduce the risk of passing HIV to partners and babies. It also covers issues once the baby is born, for example what happens if the baby is HIV positive and making arrangements to look after the baby when the mother is sick.

At the back is a list of organisations that offer help and support, plus a short list of other Terrence Higgins Trust Publications.

The author wrote the booklet in consultation with African women. It was commissioned by Enfield and Haringey Health Authority on behalf of the Department of Health, with funding also from the Inner London Health Authorities and Bristol Myers Squibb.

## Badbaadada ilmaha ee aqalka gudihisa

*See* Child safety in the home

## A beautiful smile

**FORMAT** Video, 30 min, colour
**LANGUAGE** Bengali, English, Gujarati, Hindi, Sylheti and Urdu
**AUDIENCE** Young people from the Indian sub-continent, 14–19-year-olds, Key Stage 4
**AUTHOR(S)** R. Bedi, and Centre for Transcultural Oral Health
**PRICE** £37.25 inc.
**PRODUCER** Birmingham: N Films, 1995
**DISTRIBUTOR** N Films, 78 Holyhead Road, Handsworth, Birmingham B21 0LH. Tel: 0121 507 0341; Fax: 0121 554 1872

This video aims to help young South Asian people resist the pressures of including tobacco in a betel quid or to avoid chewing betel altogether. It is targeted at 14–19-year-olds (Key Stage 4), and can be used with young people from other Black and minority ethnic communities as well as those from the Indian sub-continent.

The video uses drama and follows the story of Fatima, a 17-year-old Bangladeshi girl from Birmingham who is about to get married and is worried about paan staining on her teeth. It can be used as a trigger to encourage young South Asian people not to chew paan (lime paste, betel nut, spices, and sometimes tobacco, rolled up in a betel leaf), particularly paan with tobacco in it. The story raises a number of issues for discussion, for example, Fatima's grandmother is offended when she refuses one of her paans. Her brother does not think Fatima should criticise him for smoking as she chews paan with tobacco in it.

The programme is designed for individual or group viewing and requires basic group facilitation skills. It could be used at home or in schools, colleges and youth and community settings.

The video was produced in consultation with Sandwell Confederation of Bangladeshi Muslim Organisations and St James Advice Centre, Aston, Birmingham. The production was funded by the Department of Health.

The video is available in several languages. There are some technical problems with the English version where the English voice-over is delivered against a background of dialogue and the volume has not been lowered. This makes it confusing and in parts hard to hear.

## Big night out

**FORMAT** Video pack: video, 22 min; guide, 27-pages
**LANGUAGE** English
**AUDIENCE** 16–19-year-olds; Key stage 4
**PRICE** £66.80 inc.
**PRODUCER** Birmingham: Aquarius Education, Training and Consultancy Unit, 1994

**DISTRIBUTOR** Aquarius Action Projects,
Sixth Floor, The White House,
111 New Street, Birmingham B2 4EU.
Tel: 0121 632 4727; Fax: 0121 633 0539

*Big night out* is a young people's
multicultural alcohol trigger video aimed
predominately at young people between
the ages of 14 and 25 years. It was
produced as a three episode soap opera
tracing the experiences of a group of young
people out on a Friday night. Themes
covered are: different types of alcoholic
drink and peer pressure; the effects of
alcohol on judgement and behaviour;
alcohol and the law; and the risks and
consequences of drinking. The main
characters include a young Asian woman
and man, a young African–Caribbean
man, and young white woman and man.

The user guide is in two parts. Part one
provides tips on using the video and
preparation for dealing with issues raised in
the video. These include swearing, racism,
sexism and sexual health. Guidance is
given to trainers on how to deal effectively
with these issues as they arise in training.
Trainers are reminded that the National
Curriculum requires school and college
guidelines to be followed in the treatment
of the sexual health section.

Part two includes a synopsis of each
episode accompanied by an outline of the
aims, objectives, trigger questions, points
of issue and suggestions for follow-up
work with young people. The user guide
is clearly written and well laid out. With
careful preparation of the materials
provided, workers new to training would be
able to run well presented workshops. The
pack does not provide basic information
about alcohol issues but does provide a list
of useful addresses including details of an
extensive specialist library on alcohol issues
and an agency offering resources
specifically aimed at young people.

The video is designed for use with groups
of young people in formal and informal
settings such as schools, colleges and youth
centres. The video is interesting, relevant
and creative and uses realistic dialogue and
setting. The user guide gives useful training
support. The pack will be welcomed as it is
especially useful for work with Asian and
African–Caribbean young people as they
are represented in the video, and for anti-
racist youth work.

This video pack was developed and
produced with financial assistance from the
Alcohol Education and Research Council,
Charity Projects, Dudley District Health
Authority, Health Education Authority
(Regional Alcohol Coordinators' Support
Scheme), Urban Programme (Dudley)
and the West Midlands Regional Health
Authority. It was produced in response
to the lack of audio-visual materials that
reflect the lives and experiences of young
people in a multicultural society, especially
around alcohol related issues.

# Black and ethnic minority clients: meeting needs

**FORMAT** Video, 60 min
**LANGUAGE** English
**AUDIENCE** Health professionals, primary
health care teams, trainers, service
providers, commissioners
**AUTHOR(S)** Royal College of Nursing
**PRICE** Not for sale – available for preview
at viewing centres nationally
**PRODUCER** London: Healthcare
Productions, 1993
**DISTRIBUTOR** Available for preview at
viewing centres nationally

This video for nurses, midwives and health
visitors aims to inform about the need for,
and role of linkworkers and advocates in
assisting communication between health

professionals and patients. It was made for the *Update* series which is part of the Royal College of Nursing's Continuing Education Project for nurses, midwives and health visitors and is supported by the Department of Health.

A dramatised sequence demonstrates how difficult it is for patients and health professionals to communicate if they do not have a shared language. Linkworkers and advocates explain their role and the contribution they make to effective communication. How to work with a linkworker is explored. Issues such as matching linkworkers and patients appropriately, planning, body language during consultations, directing questions to the patients, allowing enough time for linkworkers to explain as well as translate are covered. Consultations involving linkworkers are seen in action with the linkworkers explaining cultural, religious and other factors to health professionals and explaining agency systems and practices to patients. It stresses that linkworkers are trained professionals who can contribute to uptake of services and compliance with treatment as well as help ensure a more equal service for all.

The video is not for sale but can be seen at viewing centres around the country. Health professionals will find this an informative video and linkworker schemes may wish to use it with health professionals to explain what a linkworker can do and how to work together.

## The body map

**FORMAT** Pack unpaged, illustrated
**LANGUAGE** Arabic, Bengali, Farsi, English, French, Gujarati, Punjabi, Somali, Tamil and Urdu (in one volume)
**AUDIENCE** Primary health care workers, community workers, patients

**PRICE** £15.00 inc.
**PRODUCER** London: Multi-Link Multicultural Services, 1997
**DISTRIBUTOR** Multi-Link Multicultural Services, 5 Alexandra Grove, London N12 8NU. Tel: 020 8445 5123

*The body map* is for GPs, community workers, health workers and patients. The pack includes 12 colour illustrations of the body, skeleton and organs with over 100 medical terms and other associated words.

The pack is in two sections, male and female, each with six colour postcard-size drawings. Both male and female drawings contain illustrations of a clothed person, front views, back bone structure, body organs and reproductive organs. The male drawing also includes a skeleton, and the female one includes a pregnant woman.

On the flip side of each illustration are six associated words in English with a translation of the above languages. There are 48 additional words frequently used by patients and GPs, such as 'coughing', 'itching' and 'sore'.

The pack may be most useful when working with an individual in preparation for a hospital, clinic or GP visit. It could be used to assist interpreters in supporting patients.

## Boys on the game

**FORMAT** Video, 30 min
**LANGUAGE** English
**AUDIENCE** Health care professionals, sexual health agencies, youth and community workers
**PRICE** £65.00+VAT+p&p
**PRODUCER** London: BBC, 1993
**DISTRIBUTOR** BBC Videos for Education and Training, 80 Wood Lane, London W12 0TT. Tel: 020 8576 2541; Fax: 020 8576 2916

This video is the first programme in the BBC TV series *All Black*, produced in 1993. The documentary examines the rise of young African–Caribbean men involved in selling sex. The young men talk anonymously about the reasons for their involvement in prostitution. Black workers from health agencies offer their analysis of this relatively recent phenomenon. This includes economic necessity, involvement with alcohol and drugs, and the damage caused by living in a racist society. Wider issues, such as the myths about black men's sexuality and the desires of mostly white middle-aged 'punters', are considered. The health workers also explain the health risks and risk of violence that these young men face.

The video offers some information about the kinds of services that some agencies offer, for example, counselling, health promotion and health care, from a black perspective. It acknowledges how difficult it is for young black men to access services.

Restricted for education and training purposes, this video could be used with groups of young people in youth settings, with parents in community settings, or with health care workers especially those working in sexual health services. Notes are not provided with the video, and facilitators would need to be experienced in working with groups and in dealing with sensitive issues. It would be necessary to supplement the information with details of services available to this group. Sometimes the picture quality is poor owing to the use of night shots, although the pictures are not essential to the key points raised.

# Breast screening training pack for minority women

**FORMAT** Pack, 150-pages
**LANGUAGE** English (African–Caribbean version), Bengali, Cantonese, Gujarati, Hindi, Punjabi, Urdu and Vietnamese
**AUDIENCE** Health professionals, black and minority ethnic women
**AUTHOR(S)** C.L. Fong and D. Knight
**PRICE** £30.00+p&p
**PRODUCER** Leeds: Leeds Health Promotion Service, 1994
**DISTRIBUTOR** Leeds Health Promotion Service, St Mary's Hospital, 3 Greenhill Road, Armley, Leeds LS12 3QE.
Tel: 0113 2790121 ext 4589

This pack for women and health professionals aims to develop good practice guidelines in the delivery of breast awareness training for black and minority ethnic women. There are versions for: African–Caribbean, Bengali, Chinese and Vietnamese, Gujarati, Hindi, Punjabi and Urdu women.

The pack was produced as part of a two-year research project funded by the National Health Service Breast Screening programme and produced by Leeds Health Promotion Service. Minority ethnic women were identified and trained as community health educators in order to deliver breast screening training programmes over a 50-hour period to their respective communities. The content of the pack is based on the evaluation of this project. The pack is not intended to provide detailed medical information about breasts or breast cancer but is a training resource to raise breast awareness.

The training is divided into five sections: breast health and breast screening; health education in the community; effective community health educators; training aids; and further information. It is a comprehensive and easy to use pack although it requires preparation time and training prior to delivery.

The pack includes an audio-cassette covering practical information about breast screening, 15 overhead transparencies, resource sheets and over 30 exercises to use with participants.

The cassette aims to raise discussion about breast screening and contains a conversation between two women, one of whom has been to a breast screening mobile unit. The other woman has just received an appointment to attend. It aims to raise discussion around breast screening, for example support and fear. One side of the cassette reflects thoughts of women and men on women's health and the need for screening. The cassette relates directly to the exercises in the pack. These are set out clearly with the aim, material needed, method and points for discussion. The exercises include such issues as risk factors, images of cancer, and a number of warm-up and group exercises. A photographic story with brief captions shows a woman going through the breast screening procedure. This is another useful method to use with participants.

# Call for care

**FORMAT** Book, 64-pages
**LANGUAGE** English, Gujarati, Punjabi and Urdu
**AUDIENCE** South Asian carers of older people
**PRICE** £1.95+£0.80 p&p
**PRODUCER** London: Health Education Authority and King's Fund Centre, 1994

**DISTRIBUTOR** Health Education Authority Customer Services, Marston Book Services, PO Box 269, Abingdon, Oxon OX14 4YN. Tel: 01235 465565; Fax: 01235 465556

This book, produced by the Health Education Authority and King's Fund, is for South Asian carers of older people. It provides information about sources of help and support for carers, as well as tackling more difficult issues such as emotions and death.

The book begins by defining 'carers'. Services that may be available to help carers, including welfare benefits, are described. Consideration is given to communication difficulties, and sample letters in English requesting interpreting services are included. Much of the advice is practical, with addresses and suggestions about how to take action, case studies and comments from carers illustrating points throughout.

The book notes how carers may have mixed feelings about the person they care for and may have to cope with difficult behaviour. Some carers may find it a relief to read that other people also feel the same way. Stereotypes of South Asian families as always close-knit and supportive are challenged and there is advice about how to campaign for more equal services that respond to the needs of Asian communities.

Carers will find this a useful and interesting book. Those who are unsure of what they can ask for or are entitled to will find it a helpful guide, as will those who work with carers.

# Calling all women: health checks that can save your life

**FORMAT** Booklet, 6-pages, illustrated
**LANGUAGE** Bengali, Chinese, English, Gujarati, Hindi, Punjabi, Somali, Turkish, Urdu and Vietnamese
**AUDIENCE** Women
**PRICE** £0.20
**PRODUCER** London: Women's Nationwide Cancer Control Campaign, 1994
**DISTRIBUTOR** WNCC, Suna House, 128/130 Curtain Road, London EC2A 3AR. Tel: 020 7729 4688; Fax: 020 7613 0771

This booklet, available in a number of languages, gives women practical information about the cervical smear test, breast awareness and breast screening by mammography. It was funded by the Department of Health.

The booklet answers common questions such as does a smear test hurt, why might a repeat smear be needed, what changes to look for in the breast, and how is a mammogram taken. It emphasises that early detection gives the best chance of a cure and that the tests are free. Women who have any questions or concerns, or who notice anything different about their breasts are strongly advised to see their doctor or practice nurse.

The booklet is brightly coloured and illustrated with drawings of women of different ages and ethnic backgrounds.

The information given is clear and frank but the booklet would benefit from a short introduction, outlining the facts about breast and cervical cancer, and putting information about the tests into context.

# Caring for other people's children: a guide for private foster carers

**FORMAT** Pack, 39-pages, illustrated
**LANGUAGE** English
**AUDIENCE** Private foster carers and professionals working with such carers and families of black children
**AUTHOR(S)** Health Visitors' Association and Private Fostering Special Interest Group. Editor/chair: D. Batty
**PRICE** £2.50+p&p
**PRODUCER** London: BAAF, 1995
**DISTRIBUTOR** British Agencies for Adopting and Fostering, Skyline House, 200 Union Street, London SE1 0LX. Tel: 020 7593 2000; Fax: 020 7593 2001
**ISBN** 1873868235

This pack aims to help all foster carers who look after children of a different ethnic origin from their own, particularly private foster carers of West African children, to understand and enjoy this experience. It provides information on caring for West African children.

As well as giving practical information, this guide also raises awareness of cultural issues – for example that the concept of adoption, where all family ties are broken, is a particularly European one. There are chapters on: the law and private fostering; settling the foster child into his or her new home; black children and identity; and looking after the child's health, skin and hair. There is also a chapter on West African food including some recipes.

Appendices on circumcision (male and female), sickle cell disorders, Hepatitis B infection and HIV/AIDS are provided. There are lists of organisations that provide general information, books and toys, and cosmetics and hair products. References and suggestions for further reading are included at the end of each chapter.

The guide is addressed directly to the foster carer and can be used for personal reading or reference. At the back, it has blank pages for notes about the child and a pocket for school or medical reports. The guide would also be useful to those people thinking about becoming private foster carers, and as a source of background information for health visitors, social workers and other primary care workers who work with private foster carers and families of black children.

It is clearly set out, and sensitive issues are thoughtfully discussed. The material would need updating if, for example, there were changes in legislation.

The Department of Health contributed towards the production of the guide and the authors welcome comments about it.

# Caring for patients. A multi-cultural illustrated guide

**FORMAT** Book 48-pages, colour, illustrated
**LANGUAGE** Arabic, Bengali, Chinese, English, French, German, Greek, Gujarati, Hindi, Italian, Polish, Punjabi, Spanish, Turkish and Urdu (all languages in one book)
**AUDIENCE** Patients, health care professionals, primary health care teams
**PRICE** £12.00
**PRODUCER** London: Health Education Authority, 1995
**DISTRIBUTOR** HEA Customer Services, Marston Book Services, PO Box 269, Abingdon, Oxon OX14 4YN.
Tel: 01235 465565; Fax: 01235 465556
**ISBN** 0752103024

This book aims to provide medical staff and non-English speaking patients with a simple means of communication. It contains pictures with translations for health care professionals and patients to communicate about symptoms, requirements and procedures. The guide was published by the Health Education Authority in association with Help the Hospices.

Essential phrases are given in 15 languages with a selection of drawings illustrating medical symptoms, requirements and procedures. A typical page gives a short phrase, for example 'I want', in each of the languages, together with a number of vivid, clear illustrations relating to a particular topic, such as foods. The illustrations of people do not depict a wide range of ethnic groups.

Topics cover: basic personal details for registration; hospital personnel; food; drink; bodily functions; personal hygiene and grooming; correspondence; media; sleeping and sitting positions; a range of medical procedures; medication; location and intensity and factors affecting pain. A page for describing monthly periods, pregnancy and contraception, a map of the world and a labelled diagram of the human body complete this guide. Some of the illustrations are necessarily very explicit and care needs to be taken when using them, for example using same sex staff and patients.

There is no index, which may make quick referencing difficult. Nevertheless, it is a useful book covering situations most likely to occur in hospital contexts. Its use would undoubtedly relieve some of the anxiety that the patient and medical staff could experience where they do not have a shared language for communicating medical needs and care.

# Challenging racism (CEDC)

**FORMAT** Pack, 36-pages, illustrations, tables
**LANGUAGE** English
**AUDIENCE** 14–16-year-olds, Key Stage 4, 16+ years, teachers, youth workers
**PRICE** £17.50 inc.
**PRODUCER** Milton Keynes: The Chalkface Project, 1993
**DISTRIBUTOR** The Chalkface project, PO Box 907, Milton Keynes MK13 8YU. Tel: 01908 505151; Fax: 01908 504020

This pack is for use with Key Stage 4 students and young people. It aims to provide opportunities for young people to explore their perceptions of, and attitudes towards, people from different cultures and races. It was produced by the Chalkface Project.

The pack consists of 28 activities designed for personal and social education and English classes but which can also be used for humanities and tutorial work. Each one-page activity is illustrated and can be photocopied. Most of the activities are designed for completion in a single lesson and there are suggestions for homework and extension activities. The activities encourage students to develop more thoughtful attitudes and to challenge racism. They range from less risky to more risky and offer a mix of individual and small group work.

The pack also contains notes for teachers. These advise users to be aware of the students' attitudes before using the pack and suggest that they may be more appropriate for a mature group with whom the teacher/presenter has a good relationship. A section at the end provides more information about each activity.

Although designed for classroom use this pack could be used in many other settings such as youth clubs. It is a flexible resource that could be used in its entirety or selectively according to the time available. The producers note in the introduction that classes in which one racial or cultural group are a minority will need careful management, guidance is not offered about how to do this apart from brief comments in the teachers' notes.

# Challenging racism (Independence Educational Publishers)

**FORMAT** Pack, 40-pages, illustrated, tables
**LANGUAGE** English
**AUDIENCE** 16–19-year-olds, Key stage 4, teachers
**AUTHOR(S)** C. Donellan (ed.)
**PRICE** £5.95+p&p
**PRODUCER** Cambridge: Independence Educational Publishers, 1997
**DISTRIBUTOR** Independence Educational Publishers, PO Box 295, Cambridge CB1 3XP. Tel: 01223 566130; Fax: 01223 566131

This pack is the sixth volume in a series, *Issues of the nineties*. The series aims to offer up-to-date information about important issues in our society and this pack examines the issues of racial discrimination and racial violence. A set of study guides, called 'Exploring the issues' accompanies this series.

Racial discrimination examines the issues of racism and racial violence. The pack contains reprinted articles, an index and a list of further resources. The articles come from a variety of sources including government reports and statistics, newspaper reports and features, magazine articles, surveys, literature from lobby groups and charitable organisations. It is hoped that the reader will critically evaluate the information, deciding whether material is biased/unbiased, fact/opinion, and develop their own views. Readers will have to discern the difference between the views of the writers and the complex reality for the communities being described. For example, assertions that black people hate being called British, imply that this view is shared by the majority if not all, and must be viewed with caution.

It is a starting point for accessing information about the many issues involved. Some assignments require further reading and research and readers would do well to investigate the historical and contemporary writings of black and minority ethnic scholars and researchers who have uncovered little known facts about the history of the presence of black peoples in Britain, their contribution to civilisations globally, and some of the more dynamic contemporary theories of cause and effect of racial discrimination in contemporary British society.

An accompanying study guide suggests a wide range of assignments and activities for personal and social education and associated curricular areas on GCSE, A-level and GNVQ Further and Higher Education courses. Schools and colleges might find this useful in developing an understanding of discrimination and as a resource for social sciences courses. When used with groups, the pack requires basic group facilitation skills.

# Child safety in the home

**VARIANT TITLE** Badbaadada ilmaha ee aqalka gudihisa
**FORMAT** Video, 13 mins 14 seconds (English dubbed version)
**LANGUAGE** Bengali, Somali, Turkish and Urdu (all with English dubbing in second part of tape)
**AUDIENCE** Parents, black and minority ethnic groups, health visitors, safety officers, community groups
**PRICE** £20.00
**PRODUCER** London: East London and City Health Promotion, 1997
**DISTRIBUTOR** Community Relations and Health Promotion, East London and The City Health Authority, Aneurin Bevan House, 81–91 Commercial Road, London E1 1RD. Tel: 020 7655 6600; Fax: 020 7655 6666

This two-part video is aimed at parents and carers and deals with child safety in the home and preventive measures.

The first part of the video, lasting eight minutes, covers burns and scalds. It explores day-to-day hazards and accidents, and how to avoid them. These include:
● portable and fixed fires, fireguards and unattended fires;
● burning incense safely;
● trailing flexes on kitchen equipment;
● cookers, ovens, hobs, pots, pans and frying;
● hot food and beverages;
● electrical sockets and socket covers;
● smoke alarms;
● high chairs, safety harnesses and safety gates;

bathing children, hot water taps, testing water temperature and leaving a child unattended by an adult.

The second part of the tape lasts for five minutes and covers: falls; suffocation and choking; cuts and poisoning. The topics include:

- fixing corner guards to furniture;
- fixing window locks and ensuring child-safety near open windows;
- door locks being out of children's reach;
- covering glass door panels with plastic, safety film;
- ensuring small household objects are out of reach to toddlers;
- never giving babies or toddlers peanuts, hard or chewy sweets;
- keeping cleaning products out of children's reach and fitting cupboard locks to doors and fridges;
- keeping tablets and medicines away from children;
- ensuring all sharp objects are safely stored;
- professionally fitting and always using child's car seats and harnesses.

The video suggests parents and carers talk to their health visitor or child safety officer if they have any queries over child safety and ask for support from the home safety loan scheme if they cannot afford to purchase items of safety equipment.

The video can be viewed by parents on their own but would be most effective if used by a facilitator as part of a child safety session for parents. Facilitators could make available information about local contacts and sources of help.

# Chinese oral health education materials

**FORMAT** Pack: A2 colour poster; A4 folded leaflets, colour x 3
**LANGUAGE** Chinese and English
**AUDIENCE** Dental health providers, Chinese community
**PRODUCER** Leeds: Oral Health and Ethnicity Unit, University of Leeds, 1997
**DISTRIBUTOR** Leeds Dental Institute, Clarendon Way, Leeds LS2 9LU. Tel: 0113 233 6181; Fax: 0113 233 6140 (contact Stella Kwan)

This pack, developed for the Chinese community, aims to promote and encourage good dental hygiene and practice. It is suitable for use with all ages.

The pack was produced by the Oral Health and Ethnicity Unit at the University of Leeds, and designed by Chinese Marketing and Communications. The pack is supported by the Department of Health.

The pack consists of an A2 colour poster in Chinese with English translation. This depicts a Chinese family above five basic dental health messages: brush your teeth thoroughly everyday; use a fluoride toothpaste; visit the dentist regularly; reduce the frequency of sugar intake between meals; and ask your local water company to fluoridate water supplies.

The three accompanying leaflets are entirely in Chinese, with only the title translated in English. The issues covered are: visiting the dentist; losing teeth; and caring for your teeth and gums during pregnancy. They are illustrated with drawings and real life pictures of teeth and gums.

The leaflet about visiting the dentist includes information about available dental treatment, both NHS and private. It would be advisable to check that the printed information is current.

# Combating racial prejudice against Irish people

**FORMAT** Pack, 32-pages
**LANGUAGE** English
**AUDIENCE** Early years workers – teachers, trainers, social workers
**PRICE** £5.00+p&p
**PRODUCER** Wallasey: EYTARN, 1994
**DISTRIBUTOR** Early Years Trainers Anti-Racist Network, PO Box 28, Wallasey, L45 9NP. Tel/Fax: 0151 639 6136

This resource aims to train early years workers to understand and identify prejudice against Irish people and work effectively in partnership with parents to develop a positive childcare environment for all children. It is produced by the Early Years Trainers Anti-Racist Network (EYTARN). There is a complementary pack about racial prejudice and Jewish people.

The introduction summarises the arguments in favour of extending the definition of racism to include Irish people, such as their history of institutionalised oppression, and arguments against, for example, that Irish people experience white privilege. The pack outlines the history of and rationale for the inclusion of Irish people within the Race Relations Act 1976. It also gives a historical synopsis on The Irish Experience and contemporary issues in Irish people's experience of prejudice in employment and housing in Britain.

The training addresses five themes: ourselves and people different from

ourselves; our feelings and other people's feelings; label containers, not people; using the law; and partnership for equality. A mix of role-play, games, group brainstorms, case studies, structured discussions and triggers are provided. The exercises were based on issues that arose in practice and provides a realistic focus for training development. Trainers' notes include aims but not the timing of exercises. Preparation by trainers will need to include careful consideration of debriefing approaches to suit the diversity of the group with whom they may be working.

Early years education specialists and trainers, policy advisors and training organisations will find many useful exercises in this resource. It is suitable for training childcare workers, teachers, play therapists, childminders and others involved in developing children and resources for work with children. Trainers may find that their perspectives on racism need to be thought through in the light of the perspective of racism underpinning this resource.

# Combating racial prejudice against Jewish people

**FORMAT** Pack, 32-pages
**LANGUAGE** English
**AUDIENCE** Early years workers – teachers
**PRICE** £5.00+p&p
**PRODUCER** Wallasey: EYTARN, 1994
**DISTRIBUTOR** Early Years Trainers Anti-Racist Network, PO Box 28, Wallasey L45 9NP. Tel/Fax: 0151 639 6136

This resource aims to train early years workers to understand and identify prejudice against Jewish people, work effectively in partnership with parents to eliminate negative practices and attitudes towards Jewish people and develop positive childcare environments for all children. It is produced by the Early Years Trainers Anti-Racist Network (EYTARN). There is a complementary pack about racial prejudice and Irish people.

The introduction presents the arguments in favour of extending definitions of racism to include the experiences of Jewish people, such as their history of institutionalised oppression, and arguments against, for example, that Jewish people experience white privilege. It summarises the history of the inclusion of Jewish people within the Race Relations Act 1976 and establishes the principle. It concludes with recommendations for Partnership for Equality and Working for Change.

The chapter on 'The Jewish experience' provides explanations for: anti-Judaism – hostilities towards Jewish beliefs and practices; anti-Semitism – prejudice and discrimination directed at Jewish people; and anti-Zionism – opposition to the Israeli government. A historical overview of the prejudice experienced by Jewish people includes their expulsion from Britain in 1290, Jews as subjects of the first immigration laws in Britain in 1905, the 1930s Black Shirt movement and public support of Hitler's anti-Semitism by members of Britain's Parliament. Contemporary experiences of racism are also included.

The training covers five themes: ourselves and people different from ourselves; our feelings and other people's feelings; label containers, not people; using the law; partnership for equality. A mix of role-play, games, group brainstorms, case studies, structured discussions and triggers are provided. Trainer's notes include aims but not the timing of exercises. Preparation by trainers will need to include careful consideration of debriefing approaches to suit the diversity of the group with whom they may be working.

All of the exercises are based on issues taken from practice and reflect Jewish experiences. They provide a realistic focus for training development. The focus of this training resource moves from identifying issues and underlying feelings to practical approaches for implementing improved practices.

Early years education specialists and trainers, policy advisors and training organisations will find many useful exercises in this resource. Suitable for training childcare workers, teachers, play therapists, childminders and others involved in developing children and resources for work with children. Trainers may find that their perspective on racism needs to be thought through in the light of the perspective on racism underpinning this resource.

# The cost of smoking

**FORMAT** Video, 13 min; leaflet
**LANGUAGE** Bengali and Somali with English subtitles
**AUDIENCE** Male Muslim smokers
**PRICE** £32.00 inc. (NHS). £32.00+VAT (non-NHS)
**PRODUCER** London: East London and the City Health Promotion, 1996
**DISTRIBUTOR** Community Relations and Health Promotion, East London and The City Health Authority, Aneurin Bevan House, 81–91 Commercial Road, London E1 1RD. Tel: 020 7655 6600; Fax: 020 7655 6666

The video aims to encourage male, Muslim smokers to quit. It explores the reasons for smoking and for giving up and suggests that Ramadan is an ideal time to give up for good. The two language versions of this video (Somali and Bengali) are virtually identical visually and in the text. The first features members of the Somali community and the latter members of the Bangladeshi community in London.

The video raises awareness and gives information to back-up why smokers should quit, concentrating on financial reasons, health, family well-being and views on smoking within Islam.

It features Somali/Bangladeshi male adult smokers and those who are thinking of giving up or have done so. It includes interviews with male health professionals, including a religious representative and a doctor from the same community.

There is a leaflet in English for those using the video, who are most likely to be primary care workers, health advocates, community workers, teachers and trainers/facilitators.

The leaflet emphasises the need for a group discussion following the showing, and summarises key facts and figures from the video. It also provides extra information, for example on smoking and Islam, and suggests a basic strategy for those thinking about quitting.

Those workers who will be showing the video should have appropriate information available on stopping smoking and sources of local support. They should be prepared to provide further explanation on any of the subjects that are mentioned in the video, such as cot death, addiction and withdrawal, various cancers and nicotine replacement.

The video is well-produced and could be a useful introduction to a discussion on giving up smoking.

# Current treatments for HIV: a guide for African communities in the UK

**FORMAT** Booklet, 40-pages
**LANGUAGE** English and French
**AUDIENCE** African communities in the UK
**AUTHOR(S)** J. Ochieng and E. King
**PRICE** Single copies free
**PRODUCER** London: Health First, 1998
**DISTRIBUTOR** Health First, Mary Sheridan House, 15 St Thomas Street, London SE1 9RY. Tel: 020 7955 4366

This booklet in English and French is aimed at African people living in the UK who have been diagnosed as having HIV. It provides information about current treatments, how to access them and about maximising health.

Chapter one provides the background and chapter 2 gives some basic information about HIV and AIDS, for example, the booklet explains what they are, how HIV is transmitted and how it effects the body. In chapter 3, the booklet discusses HIV testing and dealing with a positive result, including talking to someone about this. The next chapter raises family issues, in particular telling a partner and your children.

Chapters 5 to 11 provide information about medical services, standard medical monitoring, treatment options, an overview of illnesses, reducing woman-to-child transmission, treatments for children and clinical trials. Although written clearly, the information is detailed and some people may find it difficult to understand without help or further explanation. For example, it describes the range of current anti-HIV drugs being used. There is a glossary at the back that explains some of the terms used.

The booklet could be used to support counselling and consultations as well as for individual reference.

Chapter 12 provides information about healthy living and what people with HIV can do to keep well. This includes diet, safer sex and drug use and receiving community support to manage at home. The final two chapters provide details of advice and advocacy services and what they can offer.

# Cystic fibrosis: diagnosis and adolescence

**FORMAT** Audio-cassettes x 2, transcripts x 3
**LANGUAGE** Cassettes in Gujarati and Urdu, with English transcripts
**AUDIENCE** Health professionals, social workers, parents
**PRICE** Free
**PRODUCER** Bromley: Cystic Fibrosis Research Trust, 1993
**DISTRIBUTOR** Cystic Fibrosis Research Trust, Alexander House, 5 Blyth Road, Bromley, Kent BR1 3RS.
Tel: 020 8464 7211

These audio cassettes are primarily for parents of children with cystic fibrosis but will also be of interest to other family members and carers. One cassette covers diagnosis and issues for babies and children, the other cassette covers adolescence and issues parents may face as their children approach adulthood. They were produced by the Cystic Fibrosis Trust with funding from BBC Children in Need and the Department of Health.

The cassettes consist of a discussion between a doctor, facilitator and parents. The diagnosis cassette covers basic information about cystic fibrosis and answers common questions about life expectancy, range of severity, treatment,

diet, immunisation, coping with school, support groups and financial help. The discussion tackles not only factual information but also suggestions for dealing with difficulties such as children refusing to eat. Emotions and feelings are also addressed such as relationships with siblings and fitting in at school.

The adolescence cassette seeks to cover the worries parents may have as their child grows up. Young people's non-compliance with treatment is discussed (diet, medication and physiotherapy), looking at it from the young person's point of view and encouraging parents to be honest and supportive with the young person. It stresses that many children with cystic fibrosis are now reaching adulthood and parents have at some point to step back so that the young person can take on the responsibility for his or her treatment.

These cassettes are informative but also acknowledge the fears and worries parents have. They encourage parents to ask questions of professionals if they do not understand something or need more information. The value of support groups is mentioned and parents are encouraged to make contact. The cassettes are based on interviews with parents of children with cystic fibrosis and doctors who work with families from Asian communities.

# Damage caused to the body by diabetes

**FORMAT** Video, 8 min
**LANGUAGE** Bengali, with and without English sub-titles
**AUDIENCE** Bengali-speakers with diabetes; primary health care teams
**PRICE** £15.00 inc. or £10.00 hire (3-day preview)
**PRODUCER** London: East London and The City Health Promotion, 1994

**DISTRIBUTOR** Community Relations and Health Promotion, East London and The City Health Authority, Aneurin Bevan House, 81–91 Commercial Road, London E1 1RD. Tel: 020 7655 6600; Fax: 020 7655 6666.

This video aims to inform people with diabetes about how to prevent or reduce damage that could be caused by it. The video is part of a series for Bengali communities on various aspects of diabetes care. It was produced by East London and the City Health Promotion Service worker specialists in diabetes and nutrition at the Royal London Hospital NHS Trust.

In four sections, the video uses a voice-over format and various people to illustrate prevention and reduction of potential damage to eyes, kidneys, feet and heart caused by diabetes. Effective management of diabetes treatment through diet, blood and urine testing, record keeping and regular medication as prescribed, is stressed throughout. The importance of annual medical checks and the danger of delay in seeking medical advise are reinforced. The causes of damage to the body and likely medical remedies are mentioned. A checklist on the care of feet is given and the factors increasing the risks of heart attack are covered.

The video was designed for use by health professionals with groups and individuals to trigger discussion and enable more effective control of diabetes to minimise risk of damage. The video was made in response to the needs of the local community.

# Diabetes: a guide for African–Caribbean people

**FORMAT** Video, 18 min; booklet, 19-pages
**LANGUAGE** English
**AUDIENCE** African–Caribbean people with diabetes, their families and carers, primary health care professionals, diabetes specialists
**PRICE** £11.95+p&p
**PRODUCER** London: British Diabetic Association, 1997
**DISTRIBUTOR** BDA Distribution Department, PO Box 1, Portishead, Bristol BS20 8DJ. Tel: 0800 585088

This short video, funded by the Department of Health, provides practical advice about diet, treatment and lifestyle for African–Caribbean people who have diabetes. It is aimed at viewers with diabetes, mainly type 2 (non-insulin dependent) diabetes, but could be used by anyone working with groups of African–Caribbean people, particularly older people, to explore individual ways of coping with the condition.

The video features three members of an African–Caribbean family who all have diabetes – Faye and Isaac Fearon who are in their fifties and their adult son Raymond. The video follows a day in their lives, and shows them at home, at work, and out and about. The family talk to the camera, to each other and to friends about the changes they have made in their lives to manage their condition. They give their own voice-over commentary. The activities covered include adjusting a Caribbean diet, shopping for food and preparing meals, weight-watching, taking exercise and foot care. It briefly covers sticking to treatment routines.

In their own words the Fearon family show how they have adapted their lifestyle and diet to control their condition. It is sympathetically filmed and the family are natural and good-humoured in the way they offer practical advice. They successfully avoid the didactic tone of some professional presenters.

The British Diabetic Association also produces a booklet of the same title for African–Caribbean people with diabetes (reviewed below) that could be used with the video.

# Diabetes: a guide for African–Caribbean people

**FORMAT** Booklet, A5, 20-pages, illustrated
**LANGUAGE** English
**AUDIENCE** African–Caribbean people who have non-insulin dependent diabetes, their families and carers; primary health care professionals
**PRICE** £1.80+p&p
**PRODUCER** London: British Diabetic Association, 1997
**DISTRIBUTOR** BDA Distribution Department, PO Box 1, Portishead, Bristol BS20 8DJ. Tel: 0800 585088

This booklet is aimed at African–Caribbean people with type 2 (non-insulin dependent) diabetes, their families and carers. Intended for individual use, it could also be used by primary health care professionals and diabetes specialists during one-to-one counselling or in diabetic clinics. The booklet could be used in conjunction with the British Diabetic Association (BDA) video (reviewed above) for African–Caribbean people with diabetes.

The booklet explains that this type of diabetes is particularly common in African–Caribbean people over 40 years of age (affecting 1 in 5). The aim of the booklet is to inform and help diabetics manage the condition and stay healthy. It explains what diabetes is, what causes it and the symptoms, how it is treated and how to reduce the risk of long-term complications.

As diet, alone or in combination with tables or insulin injections, is essential to keeping diabetes under control, this booklet offers guidance on healthy eating, with reference to traditional Caribbean foods. It also encourages diabetics to take regular activity, stop smoking and to drink alcohol in moderation.

The booklet explains about medication, hypoglycaemia, insulin teatment, complementary therapies, and the regular health checks and tests that are needed. It describes the risk of long-term complications linked to diabetes and what the diabetic can do, as well as the importance of footcare. There is advice on being unwell, driving and holidays, and the booklet highlights some aspects of religious beliefs that need to be considered, for example fasting.

The details of the BDA Careline and other publications are given at the back of the booklet, which was produced by the BDA with funding from the Department of Health.

# Diabetes: a guide for South Asian people

**FORMAT** Booklet, A5, 24-pages, illustrated
**LANGUAGE** Bengali, English, Gujarati, Hindi, Punjabi and Urdu
**AUDIENCE** South Asian people with non-insulin dependent diabetes, their families

and carers; primary health care professionals
**PRICE** £1.80+p&p
**PRODUCER** London: British Diabetic Association, 1998
**DISTRIBUTOR** BDA Distribution Department, PO Box 1, Portishead, Bristol BS20 8DJ. Tel: 0800 585088

This booklet, in five South Asian languages and English, is aimed at people from the Indian sub-continent who have type 2 (non-insulin dependent) diabetes. It is intended for their individual use and that of their families and carers, but could be used by primary health care professionals and diabetes specialists in one-to-one counselling and diabetic clinics.

The booklet explains that this type of diabetes is common in South Asian families. Its aim is to inform and help diabetics manage the condition and stay healthy. It explains what diabetes is, what causes it and the symptoms, how it is treated and how to reduce the risk of long-term complications.

The importance of diet in managing diabetes is explained and there is guidance on healthy eating with specific reference to traditional South Asian foods. The British Diabetic Association (BDA) also produces a booklet called *Healthy Asian Cooking* (also reviewed). This includes a number of traditional recipes with an alternative healthier way of preparing and cooking the dishes.

The diabetes booklet recommends seeking advice regarding religious festivals and fasting. It also promotes physical activity and exercise, giving up smoking and moderate alcohol intake for those who drink.

Treatment of diabetes with tablets is explained in more detail. The booklet also covers insulin treatment, regular checks

and testing, hypoglycaemia, and what to do if the diabetic is unwell. The long-term problems linked to diabetes are described togther with advice on how to reduce the risk, particularly the need for footcare. Diabetics who drive are reminded to inform the DVLA if they take tablets or insulin.

Details of the BDA Careline and other publications are given at the back of the booklet, which was produced by the BDA with an educational grant from a pharmaceutical company.

# Driving with diabetes and Travel and diabetes

**FORMAT** Video, 8 min
**LANGUAGE** Bengali
**AUDIENCE** Bengali speakers with diabetes and their families; primary health care teams working with this group
**PRICE** £10.00 (hire price for 3-day preview) £15.00 (to purchase)
**PRODUCER** East London & City Health Promotion, 1993
**DISTRIBUTOR** Community Relations and Health Promotion, East London and The City Health Authority, Aneurin Bevan House, 81–91 Commercial Road, London E1 1RD. Tel: 020 7655 6600; Fax: 020 7655 6666

This video contains two programmes aimed at Bengali speakers with diabetes and their families. It features Bengali speaking participants.

The first programme, *Driving and diabetes*, is three and a half minutes long. It aims to help diabetic drivers drive safely and healthily within the law. The video covers applying for a driving licence, the work of the Driver Vehicle Licensing Authority (DVLA), visiting the GP and regular medical checks.

It offers advice about the necessary precautions to take when in charge of a motor vehicle – for example, carrying glucose, sweets or biscuits in the car and avoiding alcohol prior to or during driving. The programme also explains what to do when coping with a 'hypo' whilst driving.

The second programme on this video, *Travel and diabetes*, lasts four and a half minutes and aims to reassure and to equip the diabetic traveller with hints for safer travelling. The advice includes:

- being familiar with all the equipment needed to control and manage diabetes;
- packing all relevant medication in hand-baggage that is carried with the person throughout the journey;
- consulting the relevant people prior to travelling. For example: the GP for a health check and to obtain sufficient medication; the diabetes nurse specialist for advice on obtaining an identity card to carry at all times when at home and abroad; the pharmacist for travel sickness tablets that do not clash with prescribed medications; and the airline to arrange special diabetic meals and to advise them of the condition.

The video can be used by primary health care workers with individual diabetic patients or used to facilitate group discussion during diabetic clinic sessions.

# Drugs and alcohol: a guide for Somalis

**VARIANT TITLE** Maandooriyayaasha Iyo Khamriga: wargelin – af Soomaali
**FORMAT** Booklet, 24-pages
**LANGUAGE** English (on white pages) followed by Somali translation (on pink pages)
**AUDIENCE** Somali speakers

**PRICE** Free
**PRODUCER** London: Home Office Drug Prevention Initiative, 1994
**DISTRIBUTOR** Drug Prevention Initiative, Room 354 Horseferry House, Dean Ryle Street, London SW1P 2AW.
Tel: 0171 217 8631

This booklet about drugs and alcohol is written specifically for members of the Somali communities. It could be used by individuals on their own or by an experienced facilitator to enable group discussion. The introduction highlights the increased consumption of all types of drugs, language and cultural barriers, where to go for help, reducing harm and drugs in London.

The paragraph about Drug Use in the Somali Community appreciates that, 'back home, drug use is mainly confined to marijuana smoking and chewing Qat' but that in Britain there is less restriction and drug and alcohol use is widespread.

The booklet suggests that information is important to help people make decisions, given the wide range of drugs available. Many of the more commonly available drugs are described and details are given about their effects.

The drugs covered include: Qat, stimulants: amphetamines, caffeine, cocaine, and crack; benzodiazepines (minor tranquillisers) – reference is made here to consulting your GP; opiates: heroin, methadone; hallucinogens: LSD, dance drugs: ecstasy, GHB; and other drugs: amyl nitrate, tobacco, cannabis/hashish/marijuana and alcohol.

The booklet briefly touches on the religious perspective of alcohol use with advice on confidential counselling.

A number of other issues are addressed: the dangers of mixing drugs with alcohol, injecting drugs and the legal position. There is a 'Drugs and the law' chart included in the booklet which is in English only. The advice on injecting includes the risks of HIV infection, hepatitis, septicaemia, adulterated illegal/ street drugs and 'sharing needles and syringes'. Since the booklet was produced in 1994, the advice is now not to share any injecting equipment, for example filters and water as well as 'works'.

The booklet also contains brief advice on issues for women, parents and young people. Solvents are referred to in connection only with young people.

A section of useful addresses is included but this may need to be checked in view of the age of the publication.

## Eating well: feeling good

**FORMAT** Video, 15 min
**LANGUAGE** Somali
**AUDIENCE** General public, refugees, health professionals, community workers
**PRICE** £30.00 inc.
**PRODUCER** London: East London and The City Health Promotion, 1994
**DISTRIBUTOR** Community Relations and Health Promotion, East London and The City Health Authority, Aneurin Bevan House, 81–91 Commercial Road, London E1 1RD. Tel: 020 7655 6600; Fax: 020 7655 6666

This video for Somali communities aims to inform about healthy eating and enable people to make healthy, informed choices about their diet. It was produced by the Video Production Unit of East London and the City Health Promotion Service. The video was made in conjunction with City and East London Family Health Services, the London Black Women's Health Action Project and the Royal London Hospital Trust.

The video uses a voice-over and we are told a healthy diet can be enjoyable, inexpensive and contribute to overall health. Six steps to a healthy diet are identified – eat a variety of foods, eat more fibre, eat less fat, eat less sugar, drink plenty of fluid and eat less salt. The six steps are explored in more detail with foods clearly shown and food preparation methods demonstrated. A variety of common brand-named products are shown. It is stressed that a traditional Somali diet can be very healthy and this is reflected throughout. The main points are repeated at the end of the video.

The video has been designed for use in group settings with a facilitator or health professional who can expand the information and raise other issues as appropriate. It could also be used with individuals to trigger discussion about healthy eating. The video was produced with the involvement of Somali communities and health professionals in East London.

## Enjoying our healthy food

**FORMAT** Video, 13 min; notes, 8-pages
**LANGUAGE** Pushto, Sylheti and Urdu
**AUDIENCE** Women from the Indian sub-continent
**PRICE** £37.25 inc.
**PRODUCER** Birmingham: East Birmingham Health Promotion Service, 1993
**DISTRIBUTOR** N Films, 78 Holyhead Road, Handsworth, Birmingham B21 0LH. Tel: 0121 507 0341

This video for Asian women is produced by East Birmingham Health Authority Health

Promotion Service and N Films. It is available in Urdu, Pushtu and Sylheti. A written transcription in English accompanies the video.

The aims are to raise awareness about choosing and cooking healthier food. It follows two Asian women buying, preparing and cooking food for a party at the local community centre. We see the women shopping in the local market, buying fresh vegetables and fish and discussing what they will cook. They take the food to a friend's house where she cooks a dahl and keema without using ghee. The women cook and take the food to the community centre where it is warmly received.

The main health messages put across are: try and use fresh vegetables and fruit; low fat ingredients and oil instead of ghee and butter; less salt and sugar; and more wholemeal flour and rice.

# Equal opportunities: activities for PSE and general studies in secondary schools

**FORMAT** Pack, A4 ring binder, 124-pages, illustrated
**LANGUAGE** English
**AUDIENCE** 16- to 19-year-olds; Key Stage 3; Key Stage 4
**PRICE** £47.50+p&p
**AUTHOR(S)** A. Griffith and A. Barry
**PRODUCER** Framework Press Ltd, 1995
**DISTRIBUTOR** Folens, Albert House, Apex Business Centre, Boscombe Road, Dunstable LU5 4RL. Tel: 01582 472788; Fax: 01582 472575
**ISBN** 1850081271

This pack aims to provide a series of student-centred activities on the theme of equal opportunities. It consists of an introduction and activities with student handouts.

The pack has eight units with activities on the following key areas: leisure and racism in football; citizenship and celebrating cultural diversity within communities; careers, examining the challenges that women, disabled people and ethnic minorities face entering work and within the work environment; and identity, focusing on individuality and the need to value others. These are designed to encourage students to challenge assumptions and reflect on their own attitudes.

Each unit contains tutors' notes and includes an initial activity, debrief, post-exercise activity and final task. A series of symbols indicate the nature of the task, the size of the group and approximate time needed. The student handouts follow the main units. Each session is designed to last one hour but can be adjusted according to timetabling arrangements.

The pack is designed for use in secondary schools. It employs individual and participatory methods, including simulation exercises, drama, creative writing and a board game, and requires basic group facilitation skills. Some planning and preparation work is required. For some activities it is necessary to have an audio-cassette machine and a video camera, video player and TV monitor.

The activities could form part of a planned programme of personal, social and health education (PSHE) or be delivered through cross-curricular work in a variety of subject areas. Potential users should bear in mind the proposed changes to the National Curriculum with the inclusion of 'citizenship and democracy' and PSHE.

The units focus specifically on equality issues. However, most of the black and white cartoon-style illustrations show white people and those that depict black and minority ethnic groups may be viewed by some as patronising.

# The equalizer 2: activity ideas for empowerment work and anti-racist work with young people

**FORMAT** Pack, 84-pages, illustrated
**LANGUAGE** English
**AUDIENCE** 14–19-year-olds; Key Stage 4
**PRICE** £11.00+p&p
**PRODUCER** Bristol: Bread Youth Project, 1995
**DISTRIBUTOR** Bread Youth Project, 20-22 Hepburn Road, St Pauls, Bristol BS2 8UD. Tel: 0117 942 7676
**ISBN** 0951835718

This pack aims to provide activity ideas for empowerment work with 'Afrikan Caribbean' young people and for anti-racist work with young white people.

It is designed for use by youth workers, community workers, social workers, probation workers and teachers of personal and social education (PSE). It can be used in schools, colleges and youth and community settings. The pack consists of an introduction, two sets of activities, a glossary and an evaluation.

The pack contains an introduction with facilitator's notes, activity ideas for work on anti-racism with white young people, activity ideas for empowerment work with 'Afrikan Caribbean' young people and a glossary and evaluation form.

The activity ideas explore topics such as: stereotyping; acceptable and unacceptable behaviour; identity and culture; dispelling myths and challenging misinformation; racism and society; power relationships; confronting conflict; positive images of 'Afrikan' people and achievements; and building self-esteem.

The pack contains group activities and games, including values clarification, card games, preparing Caribbean food and group quizzes. Using the pack requires basic group facilitation skills. Activities contain information on aims, resources required and method, tips on facilitating and alternative methods. Anti-racist and equality issues are comprehensively covered in this pack which was piloted with young people and youth workers in youth centres in Avon. The pack was funded by Avon County Council, Barrow and Geraldine Cadbury Trust, Greater Bristol Trust, Portishead National Trust, Save and Prosper Educational Trust and UNICEF.

# Essential Urdu/Hindi for hospitals and general practice

**FORMAT** Pack, 35-pages; audio-cassette
**LANGUAGE** Hindi and Urdu with English translation
**AUDIENCE** Health care professionals, primary health care teams
**AUTHOR(S)** L. Kaur and L. A. Parapia
**PRICE** £5.00 inc.
**PRODUCER** Bradford: Department of Postgraduate medical Education, Bradford Royal Infirmary, 1995
**DISTRIBUTOR** Department of Postgraduate Medical Education, Field House Teaching Centre, Bradford Royal Infirmary, Duckworth Lane, Bradford BD9 6RJ. Tel: 01274 364253

This book is for health professionals and Hindi and Urdu-speakers. It is essentially a glossary of Urdu and Hindi words, phrases and verbs that are likely to be used in medical settings. There is an English translation. The book aims to improve communication between South Asian patients and the medical profession. It was produced by the Department of Postgraduate Medical Education in Bradford Royal Infirmary.

The resource was developed following a short course that gave health professionals an opportunity to learn some basic vocabulary and gain an understanding of Pakistani and Indian cultures.

The book is in the style of a dictionary and includes greetings, parts of the body, prescriptions and time and days of the week. An appendix covers numbers, and vegetables and fruits, although there is no explanation as to why these particular items are included. As the booklet does not indicate how words are pronounced, there is an accompanying audio-tape that can be purchased from the Postgraduate Centre in Bradford.

The book also briefly examines some of the cultural differences between Hindus, Sikhs and Muslims, focusing on food, religion, personal habits, menstruation, contraception, birth and death.

# Food and culture

**FORMAT** Book, 44-pages, tables
**LANGUAGE** English
**AUDIENCE** Health care professionals, Primary health care teams
**AUTHOR(S)** M. De Wet, S. Jean-Marie, J. Nelson, S. Todd and T. Zaidner
**PRICE** £4.50 inc.
**PRODUCER** King's Lynn: CNG, 1995

**DISTRIBUTOR** Resource Officer, CNG, The British Dietetic Association, St James, Exton Road, Kings Lynn, Norfolk PE30 5NU

This book aims to promote awareness of the importance of food when working with different cultural groups, for example, Bangladeshi, Pakistani, Caribbean, Chinese, Greek and Greek Cypriot, Gujarati, Jewish, Punjabi, Somali, Turkish and Turkish Cypriot, Ugandan, Vietnamese and West African groups. The book is for health professionals and schools and would be particularly useful to providers and suppliers of food. It was written by five dietitians from the Community Nutrition Group and produced by the British Diabetic Association.

Divided into eight sections, the book provides basic information on food customs, including religious and cultural influences. The main food groups of different communities are detailed together with a brief glossary of common food names. The book includes a guide for producing resources, and a comprehensive reference section.

The book shows which parts of the UK have similar cultural groups and where they are represented. There is a chart detailing religious influences on diet. The religions covered are Judaism, Islam, Hinduism, Sikhism, Buddhism, Rastafarianism and Seventh Day Adventist. The chart outlines which foods are eaten and which are not, with additional comments.

It is a useful source of information for those considering producing resources or buying resources for different minority ethnic groups.

# Four by Four

**FORMAT** Pack, 18-pages, illustrated
**LANGUAGE** Bengali/English,
Gujerati/English, Punjabi/English,
Urdu/English
**AUDIENCE** Health care professionals,
teachers, youth and community workers
**PRICE** £45.00+p&p
**PRODUCER** Birmingham: Aquarius Action
Projects, 1995
**DISTRIBUTOR** Aquarius Action Projects,
Sixth Floor, The White House,
111 New Street, Birmingham B2 4EU.
Tel: 0121 632 4727; Fax: 0121 633 0539

This pack aims to provide information
about alcohol for young people and
adults from the Indian sub-continent
living in Britain.

The pack is designed to allow medical
professionals, teachers, health, youth and
community workers to print or photocopy
the information sheets to use with
individuals or groups with whom they work.

The pack comprises an introductory
A4 leaflet about using the pack, and four
A4 leaflets, entitled: 'Keeping a count on
alcohol', 'How alcohol works', 'Alcohol
and health', and 'Alcohol and the law'.
Each leaflet is in English on one side
and in one of four Asian languages on the
other side, making a total of 16 leaflets.

The introductory leaflet provides advice
to workers planning to use the pack. It
suggests a number of issues to consider,
including: researching the cultural/religious
language composition of the local South
Asian population; the importance of
not making stereotypical assumptions
regarding people's habits and behaviours;
monitoring the distribution and use of the
leaflets; how to decide whether to print or
photocopy; what ink colours are
appropriate in relation to different
religions/cultures. Further relevant
resources produced by Aquarius are
also highlighted.

The four leaflets present basic information
clearly and succinctly – each contains
approximately 10 short paragraphs in fairly
large print. For example, the information
in the leaflet 'Keeping a count on alcohol',
states what a unit of alcohol is with
examples, compares pub measures,
home measures and high strength drinks
in relation to units, and explains briefly
what low and no alcohol drinks are.

The introduction specifically highlights
issues around gender, ethnicity, age
and religion and one of the information
sheets indicates the different unit
consumption that is considered 'safe'
for men and women.

The pack was originally designed to be
used with the Aquarius alcohol trigger
video 'Sharaab' and each of the
information sheets relates to an episode
in this video. However, the introductory
leaflet states that, 'they can be used just
as effectively in their own right, as a set or
individually, either with clients or agencies
or for local distribution'. The pack could
also be used in schools and youth and
community centres.

A facilitator using this pack would
need knowledge and awareness of issues
around alcohol and alcohol misuse, as
the information provided is basic.

The pack was developed by Aquarius
E.T.C., which is the education, training
and consultancy wing of Aquarius, the
Midlands alcohol and drug agency. It is
not specified whether the pack was piloted.

# Give up smoking for the good life

**VARIANT TITLE** Sigarayi birak
yasamaya bak
**FORMAT** Video, 16 min; booklet, 10-pages,
illustrated
**LANGUAGE** Turkish with and without
English subtitles
**AUDIENCE** Smokers; primary health
care teams
**PRICE** £38.00 inc.
**PRODUCER** London: East London and
The City Health Promotion, 1994
**DISTRIBUTOR** Commercial Relations
and Health Promotion, East London
and The City Health Authority, Aneurin
Bevan House, 81–91 Commercial Road,
London E1 1RD. Tel: 020 7655 6600;
Fax: 020 7655 6666

This video aims to provide support and
ideas for Turkish people who want to stop
smoking. It looks at why people want to
stop smoking and how they go about it. It
is based around a stop-smoking group and
includes comments from other Turkish
people who have stopped smoking or
who want to stop smoking.

It depicts Turkish-speaking men and
women of all ages who are smokers but
who want to give up, or who have recently
given up. It films some of the discussion at
a stop-smoking group led by a health
worker, Demet Sun, herself an ex-smoker.

The video outlines that stopping smoking
can be difficult and can be made easier by
splitting it into three stages: deciding,
planning, and stopping. Smokers are
shown at each of these stages, talking about
their concerns and strategies for stopping.

Facts and figures about smoking-related
harm are flashed up, possibly too quickly
to be absorbed, but these are repeated
in the booklet. Some of the temporary
side-effects of stopping such as a cough,
dizziness and sleep disruption are outlined.

However, the key point that the intense
craving for a cigarette does pass off after
a few minutes is not mentioned, except
in the booklet.

The video could be used in a group
setting, with a health professional, or
viewed at home. The booklet is addressed
to the smoker thinking about stopping. It
also follows the three stages of stopping
and gives encouragement and practical
suggestions to smokers trying to quit.
Multiple copies of the booklet would be
useful if the video is used in a group.

A range of local organisations were
involved in the making of the video,
which was produced with additional
funding from Europe against Cancer.

# Good health in later life: a guide to health and social services for Bengali elders

**FORMAT** Video, 34 min; booklet
**LANGUAGE** Bengali and English (subtitled)
**AUDIENCE** Older people, carers
**PRICE** £25.00 inc.
**PRODUCER** London: East London and the
City Health Promotion, 1995
**DISTRIBUTOR** Commercial Relations
and Health Promotion, East London
and the City Health Authority, Aneurin
Bevan House, 81–91 Commercial Road,
London E1 1RD. Tel: 020 7655 6600;
Fax: 020 7655 6666

This video is a useful resource for Bengali-
speakers and their carers. It provides
straight foward information in Bengali
about how to access health and social

services for older people. It was produced by East London and The City Health Promotion, in conjunction with other local agencies and groups.

It was mainly designed for use in sessions run by facilitators but it could also be used as a stand-alone resource. It is supported by user's notes that provide additional information and pointers for further discussion. After the Bengali programme there is a short English subtitled version.

The video shows Bengali elders making use of the different services available, focusing on the health and care needs of older people. The video emphasises a positive message that good health in later life depends not only on the services available but also on older people being as socially and physically active as possible.

# Health check-up photo-pack

**FORMAT** Pack: A4 ring binder, 65-pages; 24 x A5 colour photographs; audio-cassette, 12 min
**LANGUAGE** Trainer's notes in English with key words in Bengali, Gujurati, Hindi, Punjabi and Urdu; Audio-cassette in English with introductory translations in Bengali, Gujarati, Hindi, Punjabi and Urdu
**AUDIENCE** Minority ethnic women from the Indian sub-continent, teachers/tutors of ESOL, trainers/facilitators
**PRICE** £19.95+p&p
**PRODUCER** Birmingham: H.E.A.L. Project, 1994
**DISTRIBUTOR** Resources Department, Health Promotion Service, Raddlebain Road, Selly Oak, Birmingham B29 6JB. Tel: 0121 627 8230

This pack was designed to encourage women from the Indian sub-continent to attend health checks and to enable them to become better informed about their health.

It is designed for use by a teacher/tutor or facilitator. The pack can also be used to help in the teaching of English as a foreign language. It includes brief suggestions for teaching and learning approaches to support this – for example: discussion, description, vocabulary extension, writing skills, and reading skills. Some of the exercises can be used towards accreditation on a number of listed courses.

There are ideas for using the Reader (pages 1–13 of the pack) with those students who may speak some English but need support in developing their literacy skills – for example, using flash cards, reading and repeating dialogue auditory discrimination.

The content of the Reader covers: the health check-up; making an appointment by telephone; appointment by visiting the clinic/surgery; on the check-up day; height check; weight check; blood pressure check; cholesterol check; diet; exercise; and smoking.

The text of the audio-cassette is printed in the A4 ring binder together with workshop ideas for facilitators. The content covers exactly the same health issues as the Reader but also includes the three supplementary sections from the audio-cassette. These are: the text of the health check-up Reader; getting there (following directions); learning to make an appointment (by telephone).

The pack includes some exercises and illustrated worksheets, and provides key words in English, Bengali, Gujarati, Hindi, Punjabi and Urdu for student reference and for use as flashcards. The typeface is quite small.

Twenty-four colour photographs serve to illustrate the dialogue of the audiocassette, text of the Reader and some of the group work exercises.

# Health in your hands. A guide to cervical screening

**FORMAT** Videos x 2: 4 min and 15 min; notes; 54-pages
**LANGUAGE** Arabic, English, Somali, Sylheti and Turkish
**AUDIENCE** Women; black and minority ethnic groups; health care trainers/facilitators
**PRICE** £35 (health professionals and individuals) £18.00 inc. (Community groups and people affected by cancer)
**PRODUCER** London: Cultural Partnerships, 1997
**DISTRIBUTOR** CancerLink, 11–21 Northdown Street, London N1 9BN. Tel: 020 7833 2818; Fax: 020 7833 4963 **e-mail** cancerlink@canlink.demon.co.uk

This resource is designed to help health care and community workers who work with women, particularly from the Muslim communities, to address the topic of cervical cancer and cervical screening. It aims to inform women about their bodies and to encourage them to participate in the cervical screening programme in order to reduce the number of deaths from cervical cancer.

The first, short video, is an introduction targeted at group workers. It provides useful background information and depicts women from a range of black and minority ethnic groups.

The second, longer video, is about cervical screening. It includes static photographs of women from diverse backgrounds with a voice-over commentary. Line drawings and graphics are used to illustrate the female reproductive system and the correct English terminology is clearly stated where appropriate. The script of this video is given in an appendix to the accompanying guide.

The guide for group workers provides a step by step process to help facilitators deal with issues surrounding cervical cancer and the smear test, and to make the most of the video. It contains useful information that should be read before attempting group work. Facilitators using this pack need to be aware that other sensitive topics may arise and to be prepared to deal with these. For example, issues around sexuality, morality, contraception and sexually transmitted infections.

The guide is organised in seven sections with two appendices. Section 1 is an introduction to the guide and covers the aims and objectives of the programme. Section 2, 'Learning to Run a Group', covers, knowledge, feelings, use of language, sensitive issues and general health issues. Section 3, 'Running a Group', sets out some basic guidelines for group sessions, including the venue, ground rules, and methodologies.

Section 4, 'Getting Down to Business', contains a series of exercises and activities. Details about timing and materials required for each activity are noted at the start of the exercise. Those exercises that are potentially sensitive are marked with a warning triangle '▲'. This section also contains clearly labelled illustrations of the female body. There are ideas for introducing the smear test to the group, including suggestions on allowing participants to become familiar with the speculums and spatula used during the test.

Section 5 provides factual information about cervical cancer and prevention, what happens during a smear test, results and treatments. The terms used in this pack are clearly explained in the 'Glossary' in Section 6. The final section is a list of resources.

Appendix 1 contains a multiple-choice questionnaire that group leaders can use to ensure they are familiar with the information. Appendix 2 is the video script.

The pack is culturally sensitive and attempts to take account of diversity. There is however no mention of disability.

The resource could be used in a number of ways. It could be used to train facilitators to work with groups and/or individuals in both formal and informal settings. Facilitators attempting to tackle this subject area must become familiar with the pack and this point is re-iterated several times.

# Healthy Asian cooking: a guide for people from the Indian sub-continent

**FORMAT** Booklet, 18-pages, illustrated
**LANGUAGE** Bengali, English, Gujarati, Hindi, Punjabi and Urdu
**AUDIENCE** South Asian people with diabetes, their families and carers, primary health care teams
**PRICE** £1.20 inc.
**PRODUCER** London: British Diabetic Association, 1996
**DISTRIBUTOR** BDA Distribution Department, PO Box 1, Portishead, Bristol BS20 8DJ. Tel: 0800 585088 or 01275 818700

This guide for diabetics from the Indian sub-continent was produced by the British Diabetic Association (BDA) with an educational grant from a pharmaceutical company. It is available in five South Asian languages and English. The guide would also be useful for those living with or caring for a diabetic and for health professionals working in health promotion.

The aim of the guide is to provide simple advice and recipes for a healthier diet.

The guide begins with several recommendations to help control blood glucose levels – for example, eat regular meals, eat more high-fibre foods, cut down on fried and fatty foods. Each recommendation includes examples of alternative foods, ways of cooking and relevant information. The message is that a healthier lifestyle is preferable to buying special diabetic products available commercially.

The booklet contains five traditional recipes with a healthier choice version using lower fat ingredients on the opposite page. All the recipes contain the carbohydrate and calorie content. The recipes, illustrated with a colour picture, are: cauliflower; potato and pea curry; chicken curry; mung dahl; akni (pilau); and halva.

The guide is simply written, attractive and includes further information about the BDA and its Careline. The Careline advises on all aspects of diabetes and can provide details of local branches.

# A healthy balance: a guide for parents in four languages

**FORMAT** Video, 20 min; leaflet, 4-pages, illustrated
**LANGUAGE** Cantonese, English, Gujarati and Punjabi
**AUDIENCE** Parents
**PRICE** £25.00 inc.
**PRODUCER** Nottingham: Phil Swerdlow Productions, 1995
**DISTRIBUTOR** Nottingham Community Health NHS Trust, Project Assistant, Linden House, 261 Beechdale Road, Aspley, Nottingham NG8 3EY.

Tel: 0115 942 8651; Fax: 0115 942 8606 (cheques payable to Nottingham Community Health NHS Trust)

This video aims to give basic information about weaning babies and providing children with a healthy and balanced diet. The target audience is parents who speak one or more of the languages in which the video is presented.

The first half of the video focuses on weaning. It answers the most commonly asked questions and emphasises the 'dos' and 'don'ts' of introducing babies to a range of different foods. The kinds of issues addressed include: when and how a baby should be weaned; how to introduce different textures and food groups to babies; what foods should be avoided or encouraged; and who to contact if there are concerns or questions about healthy eating.

The second half of the video looks at the content of a healthy and balanced diet for children as they are growing. The five food groups are explained and suggestions are made about selecting and combining foods.

The information is presented by an unseen narrator. The film shows mothers feeding and weaning their babies, children in a playground representing the five food groups and the buying and cooking of different sorts of food. Key questions and answers are presented in chart form.

The children and mothers in the film are from diverse cultures. There are no images of men or disabled parents or children. The video includes information about foods from a variety of different cultures. It emphasises that parents with a limited budget can still ensure that they and their children eat healthily. There is also advice on how to give vegetarian babies and children a healthy and balanced diet.

The resource could be used by parents in their own homes, by health visitors as a way of discussing the topic and by health education or community centres working with new parents. The information given is basic and it would require a facilitator who has knowledge of nutrition and diverse cultures if it is to be used as part of training session.

The video was produced by the NHS Executive Trust but does not state how it was developed or whether it was piloted.

# Healthy eating the Moroccan way

**FORMAT** Booklet, 7-pages
**LANGUAGE** Arabic with English subtitles
**AUDIENCE** General public, health professionals
**PRICE** Free
**PRODUCER** London: Parkside Community Dietetic Department, 1993
**DISTRIBUTOR** Al-Hasaniya Moroccan Women's Centre. Tel: 020 8969 2292

This booklet for Moroccan communities aims to inform people about healthy eating using traditional foods. It was made by Parkside Community Dietetic Department, Parkside Health Promotion Unit, Al Hasaniya Moroccan Women's Centre and the Look After Your Heart Community Project Scheme.

The colourful booklet uses clear photographs of traditional foods, with short sentences in Arabic and English promoting healthy eating, such as eat more fibre, and eat less sugar and fat. Advice is given about what kinds of food to eat more of, how often to eat certain foods and food preparation. It is attractive, clearly laid out and provides information about current thinking on healthy diet. The eating patterns suggested are achievable and reflect traditional foods. The booklet can be used on its own or with a health worker to discuss and illustrate healthy eating. Members of the Moroccan community were involved in the production of this booklet.

# Healthy eating for people with diabetes

FORMAT Audio-cassette untimed; advice sheet A5, 6-pages English; advice sheet A4, other languages
LANGUAGE English, Gujarati, Hindi, Punjabi and Urdu
AUDIENCE People with diabetes mellitus who speak any of the above languages; primary health care teams
PRICE £2.50+p&p (English cassette); £3.00+p&p (translated cassette); £1.00+p&p (Advice sheets)
PRODUCER London: Nutrition and Dietetic Department, Hammersmith Hospital,1995
DISTRIBUTOR Nutrition and Dietetic Department, Hammersmith Hospital, Du Cane Road, London W12 0HS. Tel: 020 8743 2030; Fax: 020 8740 3169

These cassettes aim to provide a basic healthy eating guide for people who have diabetes mellitus. It was produced by the dietitians at Hammersmith Hospital and is available in five languages.

Using a question and answer format the cassette explains diabetes and how to manage it through diet and weight loss.

Dietary advice includes eating more fibre rich food and vegetables, fish and fresh fruit, drinking more water and sugar free drinks, and finding ways to enjoy new varieties of food and drink. Practice nurses may want to supplement the information with encouragement to eat brown bread, rice, less red meat and visits to the health shop for a wider dietary choice.

The information is reassuring, brief and practical. The accompanying transcript, presented as a leaflet and written in a formal style, may be off-putting if the news of this condition is upsetting. Practice nurses may need to offer counselling, establish that users have access to a cassette player, and that leaflet print size is appropriate.

It is useful as a self-help resource or for use in a group setting for people recently diagnosed with non-insulin dependent diabetes. Primary health care workers, carers and family members would find this informative.

# Healthy eating for people who have high fat levels

FORMAT Audio-cassette untimed; advice sheet A5, 6-pages English; advice sheet A4, 3-pages other languages
LANGUAGE English, Gujarati, Hindi, Punjabi and Urdu
AUDIENCE People who have high fat levels, particularly speakers of the above languages; primary health care teams
PRICE £2.50+p&p (English cassette); £3.00+p&p (translated cassette); £1.00+p&p (advice sheets)
PRODUCER London: Nutrition and Dietetic Department, Hammersmith Hospital,1995
DISTRIBUTOR Nutrition and Dietetic Department, Hammersmith Hospital, Du Cane Road, London W12 0HS. Tel: 020 8743 2030; Fax: 020 8740 3169

These cassettes, in five languages, aim to provide a basic healthy eating guide for people who have been found to have high blood fat levels. It was produced by the dietitians at Hammersmith Hospital.

Using a question and answer format the cassette explains why it is important to reduce the amount of fat in the blood, how this affects health, and which foods help to lower the blood fat levels. Advice includes cooking with minimal fat, lowering the intake of high fat foods (chips, samosas, take-away and fast foods); increasing intake of fibre-rich foods (such as vegetables and fresh fruit), fish and starchy foods and drinking plenty of water and sugar-free drinks.

An essential take-away self-help information guide for people who have just had their blood fat measured. The cassette is particularly useful for getting the information across in a user friendly way to those who have access to a cassette player. The accompanying leaflet, which is a transcript of the cassette, is presented in a formal style, which may be off-putting if the news of the condition is upsetting.

Practice nurses may want to supplement the information with encouragement to eat brown bread and rice, less red meat and visits to the health shop for a wider dietary choice. The technical description of a high blood fat level as 5.4 mmol/l will need to be explained. Group workers, practice nurses, carers and family members would find this informative. It is useful as a self-help resource or for use in a group setting.

# Healthy eating for people who wish to lose weight

**FORMAT** Audio-cassette untimed; advice sheet A5, 6-pages English; advice sheet A4, 3-pages other languages
**LANGUAGE** English, Gujarati, Hindi, Punjabi and Urdu
**AUDIENCE** People wanting to lose weight, particularly speakers of the above languages; primary health care teams

**PRICE** £2.50+p&p (English cassette); £3.00+p&p (translated cassette); £1.00+p&p (advice sheets)
**PRODUCER** London: Nutrition and Dietetic Department, Hammersmith Hospital, 1995
**DISTRIBUTOR** Nutrition and Dietetic Department, Hammersmith Hospital, Du Cane Road, London W12 0HS. Tel: 020 8743 2030; Fax: 020 8740 3169

These cassettes, available in five languages, aim to provide a basic guide to weight loss for people who are overweight.

The relationship between diet and weight, and the type of foods that can help weight loss are explained through a question and answer sequence on the cassette. The health hazards of being overweight are explained, for example the increased risk of diabetes and hypertension, as are the benefits of losing weight such as the greater feeling of well being. Four basic points for weight loss are given: eat regularly; cut down on high energy content foods; eat more fibre-rich foods; and eat plenty of fruit and vegetables. A section on which foods could you eat without worrying, suggests drinking tea and coffee and this may need to be reviewed given the negative effects of caffeine. Regular exercise and new eating habits leading to a slow weight loss of 1–2 lbs each fortnight is encouraged.

The information is given clearly on both cassette and leaflet. It includes easily accessible and interesting material that encourages a gradual and considered approach to dieting and does not depend on expensive and fashionable forms of dieting.

It is useful as a self-help resource or for use in a group setting. Primary health care workers, carers and family members would find this informative.

# Healthy meals in Britain today: Bengali recipes

**FORMAT** Video pack: video, 16 min x 2; A4 laminated recipe sheets x 4; leaflet, 4-pages
**LANGUAGE** Bengali and dubbed English version
**AUDIENCE** Bengali community; primary health care teams; dietitians
**PRICE** £40.00 inc. (£100.00 inc. series of three
**PRODUCER** London: East London and the City Health Promotion, 1995
**DISTRIBUTOR** Commercial Relations and Health Promotion, East London and The City Health Authority, Aneurin Bevan House, 81–91 Commercial Road, London E1 1RD. Tel: 020 7655 6600; Fax: 020 7655 6666

The aim of the pack is to provide practical advice about the preparation of typical healthy meals for Bengali people. The pack was produced by the East London and The City Health Promotion in conjunction with the Royal Hospitals NHS Trust (Nutrition and Dietetics Department). One of the *Healthy meals in Britain today* series, there are also separate videos aimed at the Caribbean and Chinese communities.

The video demonstrates the preparation of the recipes. The practical and attractively presented laminated recipe cards give the same information used in the video voice-over. Where appropriate the recipes identify alternative ingredients that can be used, encourage less salt and give information about the starch and fibre contents of the meals. The recipes are for mutton curry, chapatti, flaked herring and whole green lentils with spinach. A brief resource list completes the pack.

This pack is intended to be used by facilitators who have a sound knowledge of nutrition as this is not covered in the video. It aims to encourage people to prepare traditional meals in an even healthier way. Trainers, dietitians, group workers and others with a brief to promote healthy eating will find this a practical and useful resource.

# Healthy meals in Britain today: Caribbean recipes

**FORMAT** Video, 13 min; A4 laminated recipe sheets x 4; leaflet, 4-pages
**LANGUAGE** English
**AUDIENCE** Caribbean community; primary health care teams; dietitians
**PRICE** £40.00 inc. (£100.00 inc. series of three)
**PRODUCER** London: East London and the City Health Promotion, 1995
**DISTRIBUTOR** Commercial Relations and Health Promotion, East London and The City Health Authority, Aneurin Bevan House, 81–91 Commercial Road, London E1 1RD. Tel: 020 7655 6600; Fax: 020 7655 6666

The aim of the pack is to provide practical advice about the preparation of typical healthy meals from the Caribbean. The pack was produced by the East London and The City Health Promotion in conjunction with the Royal Hospitals NHS Trust (Nutrition and Dietetics Department). One of the *Healthy meals in Britain today* series, there are separate videos aimed at the Bengali and Chinese communities.

The video demonstrates the preparation of the recipes. The practical and attractively presented laminated recipe cards give the same information used in the video voice-overs. Where appropriate the recipes identify alternative ingredients that can be used, encourage less salt and give information about the starch and fibre contents of the meals. The recipes are for steamed fish, rice and peas and vegetable one pot soup. A brief resource list completes the pack.

This pack is intended to be used by facilitators who have a sound knowledge of nutrition, as this is not covered in the video. The pack aims to encourage people to prepare traditional meals in an even healthier way. Trainers, dietitians, group workers and others with a brief to promote healthy eating will find this a practical and useful resource.

## Healthy meals in Britain today: Chinese recipes

**FORMAT** Video, 13 min x 2 Cantonese and dubbed English version; A4 laminated recipe sheets x 7 in Chinese and English; leaflet, 4-pages (English only)
**LANGUAGE** Cantonese and English (dubbed version)
**AUDIENCE** Chinese community; primary health care teams; dietitians
**PRICE** £40.00 inc. (£100.00 inc. series of three)
**PRODUCER** London: East London and the City Health Promotion, 1995
**DISTRIBUTOR** Commercial Relations and Health Promotion, East London and the City Health Authority, Aneurin Bevan House, 81–91 Commercial Road, London E1 1RD. Tel: 020 7655 6600; Fax: 020 7655 6666

The aim of the pack is to provide practical advice about the preparation of healthy typical Chinese meals. The pack was produced by the East London and The City Health Promotion in conjunction with the Royal Hospitals NHS Trust (Nutrition and Dietetics Department). One of the *Healthy meals in Britain today* series, there

are also separate videos aimed at the Bengali and Caribbean communities.

The video demonstrates the preparation of the recipes. The practical and attractively presented laminated recipe cards give the same information used in the video voice-over. Where appropriate the recipes identify alternative ingredients that can be used, encourage less salt and give information about the starch and fibre contents of the meals. The recipes are for sweet corn soup, stir-fry mange tout with baby corn, stir-fry baby cabbage with oyster sauce, steamed mackerel with ginger and spring onion and stewed chicken with chestnuts. A brief resource list completes the pack.

This pack is intended to be used by facilitators who have a sound knowledge of nutrition as this is not covered in the video. It aims to encourage people to prepare traditional meals in an even healthier way. Trainers, dietitians, group workers and others with a brief to promote healthy eating across cultures will find this a practical and useful resource.

## High blood pressure, hypertension, pressure

**FORMAT** Booklet, A5, 10-pages, colour, illustrated
**LANGUAGE** English
**AUDIENCE** African–Caribbean people
**PRICE** Free
**PRODUCER** London: HEA, 1998
**DISTRIBUTOR** HEA Customer Services, Marston Books Services, PO Box 269, Abingdon, Oxfordshire, OX14 4YN. Tel: 01235 465565/465566; Fax: 01235 465556

This booklet provides advice and guidance on hypertension for African–Caribbean people. There is an accompanying leaflet for professionals: *Hypertension and the African–Caribbean community: guidance for health professionals* (see next entry).

The booklet explains what hypertension or high blood pressure is and answers a range of commonly asked questions. Under 'How do I know if I've got high blood pressure?', the booklet describes signs, symptoms, consequences and some preventive strategies.

It includes a matter-of-fact guide to the procedure for checking blood pressure, together with information about conditions related to high blood pressure, treatment and further preventive advice.

The booklet explores 'What is a healthy lifestyle?' It suggests questions that readers can ask themselves about how they live and some positive strategies for change. For example, cutting down smoking, watching your weight and keeping fit. A height/weight chart is provided.

Healthy eating is examined in some detail, with advice on a balanced diet. It covers salt intake, fatty foods with specific mention of coconut and palm oils, and alcohol consumption. Recommended foods include fresh fruit and vegetables, starchy foods such as yam and sweet potato, and fibre from pulses like black-eyed and gungo beans.

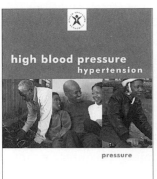

There is advice about medication, both prescribed and herbal remedies, and possible side effects. Issues for women such as the pill and pregnancy are covered. The booklet also provides a list of questions that the reader can ask their GP and concludes with suggestions for further reading.

## Hypertension and the African–Caribbean community. Guidance for health professionals

**FORMAT** Booklet, A4, 8-pages
**LANGUAGE** English
**AUDIENCE** Health care professionals, primary health care teams
**PRICE** £1.00
**PRODUCER** London: HEA, 1998
**DISTRIBUTOR** HEA Customer Services, Marston Books Services, PO Box 269, Abingdon, Oxfordshire, OX14 4YN.
Tel: 01235 465565/465566;
Fax: 01235 465556
**ISBN** 0752111183

This booklet is written for the guidance of health professionals to encourage them to consider the health needs of the African–Caribbean population in respect of hypertension because of the particular risk for this group of people. There is an accompanying booklet for the Caribbean community: *High blood pressure, hypertension, pressure* (see above).

These guidance notes provide background information about hypertension which is the leading cause of death and disability in the African–Caribbean community. A list of possible contributory factors is given. Prevention is discussed in terms of the cost of untreated hypertension. Suggestions are made for developing a screening strategy to raise awareness and encourage uptake.

Several ideas for treatment are put forward including the use of prescribed drugs, herbal remedies and advice on lifestyle.

A section on communicating with patients includes practical advice and alludes to certain cultural beliefs and attitudes. The booklet concludes by posing a series of questions commonly asked by patients.

# Hypoglycaemia and coping with diabetes during illness

**FORMAT** Video, 6 min 30 seconds
**LANGUAGE** Bengali
**AUDIENCE** Bengali speaking people with diabetes, Primary Health Care Teams working with the above group, link workers
**PRICE** £10.00 (3 day hire price – for preview); £15.00 (to purchase)
**PRODUCER** London: East London & City Health Promotion, 1993
**DISTRIBUTOR** Commercial Relations and Health Promotion, East London and The City Health Authority, Aneurin Bevan House, 81–91 Commercial Road,

London E1 1RD. Tel: 020 7655 6600; Fax: 020 7655 6666

This video in two parts is aimed at Bengali-speakers who have diabetes. The key message is the importance of monitoring diabetes and seeking help and support from health professionals. The video could be used with groups of diabetics in the Bengali community to facilitate discussion and support the management of the disease. It would be of use to diabetes nurse specialists or other primary health care professionals and link workers.

The video features Bengali speaking participants and includes still pictures and video footage with voice-over. The sound quality of the tape is poor making audibility difficult.

The first part of the tape (4 mins) concentrates on hypoglycaemia. It explains the symptoms of hypoglycaemia and diabetes, the importance of a balanced diet and the necessity for regular meals and beverages. It also explains the warning signs that precede a 'hypo' and how to manage a 'hypo'.

Coping with diabetes during illness is covered in the second part of the tape (2 mins 30 seconds). As common illnesses can affect diabetes, the video encourages the diabetic to take prompt and effective action if they are ill. This includes consulting the GP, talking to the diabetes nurse specialist, and checking with the pharmacist about over the counter medication.

# Icimizdeki duman
*See* The smoke inside us

# Immunisation: a guide for parents

**FORMAT** Video, 14 min in each language
**LANGUAGE** English, Gujarati, Hindi and Punjabi (all on one tape)
**AUDIENCE** Parents, carers, black and minority ethnic groups
**PRICE** £25.00
**PRODUCER** Phil Swerdlow Productions, 1994
**DISTRIBUTOR** Nottingham Community Health NHS Trust, Linden House, 261 Beechdale Road, Apsley, Nottingham NG8 3EY. Tel: 0115 942 8651; Fax: 0115 942 8606

This resource aims to encourage parents to have their children immunised against infectious diseases. The video also discusses travel and occupational health immunisation.

The video begins by reassuring parents that immunisation programmes are carried out around the world. It then goes on to cover a number of diseases against which immunisation offers protection. These include: diphtheria, tetanus, whooping cough, polio, measles, Hib, viral meningitis (mumps), tuberculosis and rubella (German measles).

The video highlights that while many of these diseases may not kill children they can lead to long-term damage such as: deafness, blindness, paralysis, heart problems, nerve damage, muscle spasm, bronchitis, infected ovaries, male sterility and brain damage.

The purpose of protective immunisation which is to stimulate antibodies to protect against future infections, and the methods, vaccination and oral administration, are explained. The video also covers testing and the age at which vaccinations and booster vaccines should be given.

The video explores the reasons parents give for not getting their children immunised and provides information to demonstrate why these are incorrect. Among the reasons covered are:
● thinking breast milk gives sufficient protection;
● keeping a spotlessly clean home (without considering water and air borne infection and contact with others);
● family history of epilepsy and/or asthma.

Parents are encouraged to seek advice from the GP and health visitor and to seek the services of an interpreter where necessary. The Parent Held Record of Immunisation is mentioned.

The video can be used by primary health care and community workers with parent groups to facilitate discussion around immunisation.

# Keep active, keep healthy

**FORMAT** Video, 15 min; leaflet, 4 pages
**LANGUAGE** Bengali, English, Gujarati, Hindi/Urdu and Punjabi
**AUDIENCE** Women
**PRICE** £37.25 inc.
**PRODUCER** Birmingham: N Films and UK Asian Women's Conference, 1993
**DISTRIBUTOR** N Films, 78 Holyhead Road, Handsworth, Birmingham B21 0LH. Tel: 0121 507 0341

This video for women from Asian communities promotes physical activity as a way of contributing to good health. It notes increased rates of heart disease within Asian communities compared with the rest of the population and promotes regular physical activity to help prevent heart disease. The video was made by the UK Asian Women's Conference and was funded by the Department of Health.

Throughout the video, women of all ages are seen participating in and enjoying a range of physical activities. Some are organised classes such as keep fit and aerobics, others are activities that can be incorporated into everyday life, such as using the stairs rather than the lift, walking more and stretching exercises that can be done at home. Traditional activities such as dance and yoga are included and involving the whole family in a more active lifestyle is encouraged. Women-only classes and sessions at swimming pools are noted and information is provided about what to wear for women who prefer to keep their legs covered.

A section on healthy eating advises less fat, salt and sugar in the diet. Foods to eat less of and those to eat more of are clearly shown. This includes traditional and convenience foods.

This is a stand-alone resource suitable for viewing individually or with the family at home. It is also suitable for use in group settings. It provides women with an overview of the kinds of physical activities they can do as well as reinforcing the importance of physical activity to health. The accompanying leaflet highlights the main points from the video with some useful addresses. A number of health professionals and organisations concerned with health were involved in advising the producers.

# Keep warm, keep well

**FORMAT** Booklet, 20-pages
**LANGUAGE** Bengali, Chinese, English, Greek, Gujarati, Hindi, Polish, Punjabi, Turkish, Urdu and Welsh
**AUDIENCE** Older people
**PRICE** Free
**PRODUCER** London: Department of Health, updated annually
**DISTRIBUTOR** Department of Health Distribution Centre, PO Box 410, Wetherby, West Yorkshire LS23 7LN. Tel: 01937 840250; Fax: 01937 845381

This booklet is for older people and aims to provide information and advice about how to keep warm in winter and cope with cold weather generally. It was produced as a result of a joint venture between Help the Aged, Age Concern, Neighbourhood Energy Action, Departments of Health and Social Security and the Welsh Office.

The booklet covers foods to eat, appropriate clothing and heating, paying fuel bills, welfare benefits and grants, emergencies and sources of further help and advice. The information is clear and practical, line drawings illustrate the text and there is a list of useful phone numbers at the end for people to fill in themselves. Most people will find the information helpful and relevant. Community workers may find it a support for sessions with groups of older people on coping with cold weather.

# Maandooriyayaasha Iyo Khamriga: wargelin – af Soomaali

*See* Drugs and alcohol: a guide for Somalis

# Many voices, one message: guidance for the development and translation of health information

**FORMAT** Booklet, 41-pages
**LANGUAGE** English
**AUDIENCE** Health care professionals, social workers, black and minority ethnic groups
**PRICE** £5.99
**PRODUCER** London: HEA, 1997
**DISTRIBUTOR** HEA Customer Services, Marston Book Services, PO Box 269, Abingdon, Oxfordshire OX14 4YN. Tel: 01235 465565/465566; Fax: 01235 465556

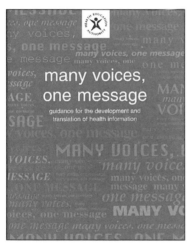

This booklet is a practical guide to developing a translation policy, producing translated materials and running translation projects. It is aimed at anyone working to adopt a multilingual approach to the provision of services and written information.

The first section covers developing a translation policy. Clearly laid out with a concise rationale, this section offers advice and information on strategies for developing a translation policy. There are points on: recognising community needs;

community involvement; building on knowledge; pooling resources; multi-agency and multidisciplinary approaches, training; standards; population size; and starting with the target audience.

The next section includes guidelines for translation, covering: interpretation and translation as communication strategies; what to translate; key features of a good translation, and bilingual, multilingual or single language.

'Producing translated materials' suggests five ways of producing documents in languages other than English. It offers guidance on clarity, mistranslation, readability, consultation, identifying content and language, piloting, dissemination and evaluation, and publicity. There is additional advice on the evaluation of health resource materials. This encourages consideration of quality and adequacy, response, uptake and impact.

There is a section on selecting and working with a translation agency. This advises what to look for when engaging translating services; for example, checking accredited qualifications, presentation brochures, and the facilities offered, such as equipment and computer software. There is guidance on appropriate language skills, the type of job, cost and proof reading.

The computer technology section highlights the issues involved in using multilingual software in a non-technical manner.
The concluding appendices cover:
● case studies that illustrate different approaches to translation;
● the results of a Health Education Authority (HEA) survey of health and related agencies;
● examples of services developed in response to need;

- a list of sources or suppliers of multilingual software;
- a list of languages mentioned by respondents to the HEA survey.

# Maternity services for Asian women

**FORMAT** Booklet, 23-pages
**LANGUAGE** English
**AUDIENCE** Health care professionals, primary health care teams, commissioners
**PRICE** Free
**PRODUCER** Leeds: NHS Management Executive, 1993
**DISTRIBUTOR** Department of Health Distribution Centre, PO Box 410, Wetherby, West Yorkshire LS23 7LN. Tel: 01937 840250; Fax: 01937 845381

This booklet for purchasers of maternity services may also be of interest to providers and users of services. It particularly addresses maternity services for women from the Indian sub-continent. It is part of a series produced by the NHS Management Executive which aims to present users' views about current services and what a quality service would consist of. The Department of Health and the Share project at the King's Fund co-operated closely in the production of this booklet.

The booklet concisely outlines current concerns about maternity services. It covers some issues specific to women from the Indian sub-continent and others relating to maternal and child health and effective use of maternity services. A longer section examines what can be done to improve services and make them more responsive to users. It includes examples of good practice from around the country and pinpoints particular issues such as promoting advocacy and making information more accessible. Throughout, quotes from women highlight the issues raised and this gives the booklet a human touch and firmly roots it in women's experience of services. There is a checklist at the end to assist purchasers to examine how maternity services are meeting the needs of all sections of the community.

This booklet is short enough to be read by everyone involved in purchasing or providing maternity services. It offers a useful basis for discussion about services and refreshingly examines services from the users' point of view.

# Meet Fatima, a girl who has HIV

**FORMAT** Booklet, 36-pages, illustrated, colour
**LANGUAGE** English
**AUDIENCE** Parents with young children; 7–14-year-olds, Key Stage 2; Key Stage 3; teachers, health care professionals working with children.
**AUTHOR** Vanguard AIDS Information Service
**PRICE** £1.50
**PRODUCER** London: Health First, 1998
**DISTRIBUTOR** Health First, Mary Sheridan House, 15 St Thomas Street, SE1 9RY. Tel: 020 7955 4366

This is an educational storybook designed for use as a learning tool. It explores the problems of telling a child about living with a life threatening illness and also the issues around prejudice and who needs to know.

It is a story about Fatima, a young, British born, African girl who is infected with HIV. Fatima, her immediate and extended family and friends are introduced throughout the story. The narrative recounts visits to the family doctor, the hospital and the specialist African health worker. School-based fears and issues and HIV education are also covered, and references made to discussions with the 'headmistress' and 'health promotion officer'.

The booklet includes explanations about HIV infection, associated illnesses, medication and the difference between HIV and AIDS at various points throughout the story. There are references to African tribal and cultural beliefs and illustrations depicting Fatima in her multicultural classroom.

The book is written in a formal literary style and could be used to facilitate discussion around HIV and AIDS with children at school and at home. It should not be used as a storybook for children to read alone.

The book contains a glossary of the words and terminology used in the story. There is also a list of useful African Community Organisations and other organisations that may be able to provide help and advice on HIV/AIDS and other health-related issues.

## Men's matters: a guide for African men on HIV and AIDS

FORMAT Booklet, 24-pages
AUDIENCE African men
AUTHOR(S) G. Kintu and L. Kawonza (ed.)
PRICE Single copies free
PRODUCER London: Terrence Higgins Trust and Innovative Vision Organisation, 1999
DISTRIBUTOR The Terrence Higgins Trust, 52–54 Grays Inn Road, London WC1X 8JU. Tel: 020 7831 0330; Fax: 020 7816 4563; Website: http://www.tht.org.uk

This booklet is aimed at African men living in the UK. It provides information about HIV based on the real life experiences of African men infected with HIV who are living in the UK.

The booklet explains what HIV is and what AIDS is, and the main routes of HIV transmission. It answers some questions about sexual practice and HIV. HIV testing is explained, specifically where to go for a test and what to expect at a clinic. The booklet highlights the issue of consent to testing, confidentiality, and pre- and post-test counselling. Under 'Thinking about an HIV test' the booklet explores the advantages and disadvantages of having the test.

The second part of the booklet provides information about the treatments for HIV and how to get support. It also explores the question of telling other people about being HIV positive.

Guidance on immigration and welfare benefits is given, including welfare, housing and income and employment benefits. Further information and advice is available from a range of services and organisations and these are listed at the back of the booklet, as well as in the text.

The booklet was written for the Terrence Higgins Trust and Innovative Vision Organisation in consultation with African men. It was commissioned by Enfield and Haringey Health Authority on behalf of the Department of Health.

## New life. A health education drama about smoking

FORMAT Video, 40 min; notes, 7-pages
LANGUAGE Video: Bengali (Sylheti dialect); notes: English

AUDIENCE Bangladeshi men and their families, friends and work colleagues; Bangladeshi speaking health workers and facilitators
PRICE £50.00 (inc. p&p) Statutory Organisations, £25 (inc. p&p) Voluntary Organisations
PRODUCER London: Confederation of Indian Organisations, working with Asian Voluntary Organisations, 1998
Distributor CIO (UK), 5 Westminster Bridge Road, London SE1 7XW.
Tel: 020 7928 9889; Fax: 020 7620 4025; e-mail: cio@gn.apc.org

This video drama raises issues about smoking and the stresses of modern life – ranging from ill health, financial hardship, passive smoking, parental influence and quitting to more general themes such as self-esteem, faith and change.

The story follows one year in the life of Harun, a Bangladeshi, who is a chef in his 40s. He is a devoted family man with a busy, stressful life and he smokes to relieve the tension. His son begins to steal money for cigarettes, his daughter's asthma is getting worse and there are problems at work. A sudden death in the family throws Harun's life into crisis. Harun battles to regain his self-esteem, a sense of purpose and tries to regain his son's respect.

This video would be most effective if used as part of a 'training' session with a facilitator to enable discussion of the issues that arise from viewing the video or that could be raised in preliminary discussions. An experienced facilitator could use this video and accompanying notes to offer support to individuals and groups who want to quit smoking, either in the workplace or in health care or community settings.

The issues raised include the appeal of smoking, the reasons people do not give up, smoking and health and how to quit smoking. Among the reasons people do not give up smoking, the video highlights stress reduction, relaxation, peer influence and pleasure. It examines why people depend on cigarettes and why smoking is so addictive.

The health problems covered include heart disease, asthma, stroke (blood pressure), cancers, respiratory diseases such as bronchitis and emphysema, and lack of energy and fitness. A number of related problems such as passive smoking, young people and smoking, and religion and smoking are covered. Alternative ways of giving up smoking are presented, including support from the family, GP and self-help groups.

# The NHS home healthcare guide

FORMAT Booklet, 64-pages, illustrated with black and white cartoon/line drawings
LANGUAGE English (also in large print and Braille), Bengali, Chinese, Gujerati, Hindi, Punjabi, Urdu and Vietnamese
AUDIENCE General public, black and minority ethnic groups
PRICE Free
AUTHOR(S) I. Banks and S. Brewer
PRODUCER Leeds: NHS Executive, HEA and Doctor/Patient Partnership, 1998
DISTRIBUTOR NHS enquiries only: NHS Response Line 0541 555455; General public – via GP surgery

This booklet is a comprehensive, step-by-step guide to self-care intended for individual use. It includes advice on treating yourself for minor ailments and how to identify the need for emergency or further treatment. It also covers how to use the available health services.

Topics covered include:
- helping your doctor to help you;
- how your pharmacist can help;
- first aid;
- a plan for healthy living;
- index of sign and symptoms;
- directory of common illnesses;
- home medicine chest;
- useful contacts and further reading.

The First aid section, written by the British Red Cross, briefly describes what to do in an emergency, including instructions for giving mouth to mouth resuscitation and the recovery position. It provides information about treating a range of injuries including: bites and stings; broken bones and dislocations; burns and scalds; choking; cuts, grazes and bleeding; fits and convulsions; head injuries; poisoning; and sprains, strains and bruises. It would not be appropriate to wait for an emergency before reading all the information contained in this section. Information about first aid training can be obtained from the British Red Cross.

Elsewhere in the guide, important/emergency information is sometimes provided in highlighted text box format.

The healthy living section contains advice and information on: smoking, 'drug abuse', physical activity, protection in the sun, mental health, sexual health, vaccinations, health screening, pregnancy; and old age. Some of the advice on alcohol consumption is placed in the healthy eating section.

The index of signs and symptoms can be used by the reader to identify common ailments and to find the relevant entry under the 'Directory of common illnesses'. The Directory is an alphabetical list of ailments and problems. For example: 'Aches and pains' covers back and neck

pain, dental pain, headache and migraine, muscle and joint pain, and colds and flu. There are sections on respiratory problems, allergies and asthma, digestive and bowel complaints, tiredness and anaemia, skin and hair problems and ear and eye complaints.

There are specific sections on common infant problems and child illnesses, women's health and men's health.

Each illness is explained briefly and there is information about signs and symptoms, causes and complications, prevention, home treatment and advice about when to consult your doctor. The reader is referred to other relevant sections where appropriate.

The small type face and dense text could be discouraging. However, it is broken up with clear headings, and several indices help the reader to find the appropriate information.

The 'Medicine chest' section covers how to keep medicines in the home and holiday health. The final section is a list of useful contacts.

The guide is intended for the general public and there are no specific references to the particular needs of different population groups.

# Oceans apart – an interactive drama and video project on HIV/AIDS for women

**FORMAT** Video pack: video, 60 min; workpack, 46-pages
**LANGUAGE** English
**AUDIENCE** Women from the black communities

**AUTHOR(S)** Black HIV/AIDS South East London and Care to Act
**PRICE** £45.00 inc. (statutory organisations); £35.00 (voluntary); £25.00 (individuals)
**PRODUCER** London: BHASEL, 1995
**DISTRIBUTOR** Black HIV/AIDS South East London, PO Box 7953, London SE4 1ZA. Tel: 020 8694 6639; Fax: 020 8694 6638

This is a training resource for black and minority ethnic women which aims to raise awareness around HIV and AIDS. It is the result of a project commissioned by Black HIV/AIDS South East London (BHASEL) and developed by Care to Act. It was funded by the London Borough of Lewisham's Women's Committee.

The resource includes a video and an educational work pack for use in a training session lasting about two and a half hours. This needs to be facilitated by someone experienced in the issues around HIV and AIDS. The video is not designed to be used on its own. The workpack provides clear guidelines for the facilitator on running a workshop, support and evaluation. It includes facts and information about HIV and AIDS, as well as useful icebreakers, games and suggestions for post-video discussion.

The video focuses on three women who meet in a gym. The women are West African, African–Caribbean and Asian. As they work out they get to know each other and eventually spend the day together talking about their lives and experiences. Their discussion on HIV and AIDS raises several issues for each of them; for example, having a relationship with a married man who is HIV positive, using condoms and female circumcision. Wider issues are also raised such as racism, being a mother, cultural differences, safer sex and heterosexism.

# One world: a race and culture activity pack for youth workers

**FORMAT** Pack: card-set, A6 activity cards x 60; booklet, 28-pages
**LANGUAGE** English
**AUDIENCE** 12–16-year-olds; youth workers
**PRICE** £9.99 inc.
**PRODUCER** Leicester: Youth Work Press/National Youth Agency, 1994
**DISTRIBUTOR** National Youth Agency, 17–23 Albion Street, Leicester LE1 6GD. Tel: 0116 247 1200; Fax: 0116 247 1043; Minicom: 0116 247 1305

The pack was designed as a creative tool to help youth workers raise young people's awareness and extend their horizons in order to develop a sense of the justices and injustices in the world. It aims to encourage young people to look beyond stereotypes and assumptions and to adopt an honest, open-minded approach to global issues in order to understand the one world ethos and their part in it.

It is a starter pack designed to generate enthusiasm and curiosity for world issues. It is flexible in its use and each activity can be adapted to suit different group interests, ages and needs. The activities are practical and can be used with groups of any size. Most of the activities are suitable for single sex or race work.

There are guidelines and notes to support youth workers in implementing the activities. They cover: establishing ground rules; challenging stereotypes, separate sex work; and doubts and questions. Each activity is clearly laid out under the headings: aims; what to do; equipment; time; and advice notes.

Activities covered include:
● An introductory ice-breaker.

- Complete the sentence: to discover how much is already known, common interests and concerns.
- Match the meaning: to promote an understanding of language, concepts and terms.
- Agree/disagree card game: to enable participants to air their views, defend opinions, and present arguments.
- Multiple choice quiz: to assess current knowledge levels, evaluate learning, give facts.
- Make a poster: a creative work activity to produce visual materials.
- Role play: to imagine and envisage a range of experiences, and explore different cultures.
- Exploring images, languages and stereotypes: to raise consciousness, analyse and ask questions and put learning into context.
- What if it happened to you?: to enable participants to explore personal involvement, structures in society and to identify cause and effect.

The booklet also contains details of other resources available from the National Youth Agency and UNICEF.

## Our Healthier Nation: a contract for health. A summary of the consultation paper

**FORMAT** Booklets: A4, 4-pages, *A contract for health: A summary of the consultation paper* (English only); A5, 5-pages plus tear off and return page
**AUDIO-CASSETTE:** side A, 7 min verbal edition of the Consultation paper summary; side B 4 min, verbal edition of the questions that appear in the A5 booklet
**LANGUAGE** Arabic, Bengali, Chinese, English, Greek, Hindi, Punjabi, Somali, Turkish, Urdu and Vietnamese.

**AUDIENCE** General public, black and minority ethnic groups
**PRICE** Free
**PRODUCER** London: Department of Health, 1998
**DISTRIBUTOR** Department of Health Distribution Centre, PO Box 410, Wetherby, West Yorkshire, LS23 7LN. Tel: 01937 840250; Fax: 01937 845381

This pack summarises the government's Green Paper on health. It offers the reader/listener the opportunity to respond to the consultation document by completing the attached questionnaire or by e-mail, although the deadline for response was 30 April 1998. The pack is for individual information although it could still be used to facilitate a group or individual responses to the Green Paper. It might also still be used to inform individuals and communities about the government's strategy as part of a community consultation exercise related to health improvement programmes or primary care groups.

The A4 summary booklet, in English only, sets out briefly the opportunities for improving people's health and the economic reasons to support the case. It puts forward the government's two key aims for health:

- to improve the health of the population as a whole by increasing the length of people's lives and the number of years people spend free from illness;
- to improve the health of the worst-off in society and to narrow the health gap.

The proposed national contract for better health is explained and the four priority target areas are outlined. These are heart disease and stroke, accidents, cancers, and suicide.

The A5 booklet and audio-cassette, available in various languages, outline the part that individuals can play in response to the Green Paper. It describes the wants and needs of the individual and discusses the shift from a negative, blaming culture to one of personal responsibility. There is also recognition of the various factors that affect an individual's health, such as poverty, unemployment, bad housing and crime.

The importance of partnership between government, local authorities, the NHS and the voluntary sector is emphasised. It also lists the settings where action to improve health can be taken, in schools, at work and at home.

# Partnership with parents: an anti-discriminatory approach

**FORMAT** Pack, 36-pages
**LANGUAGE** English
**AUDIENCE** Early years teachers, social workers, childcare providers
**AUTHOR** Early Years Trainers Anti-Racist Network
**PRICE** £5.00+p&p
**PRODUCER** London: EYTARN, 1995
**DISTRIBUTOR** Early Years Trainers Anti-Racist Network, PO Box 28, Wallasey L45 9NP. Tel/Fax: 0151 639 6136

This pack aims to provide material for childcare providers to use in developing partnerships with parents that are empowering and value diversity. The pack was produced by the Early Years Trainers Anti-Racist Network.

The resource works from the premise that discrimination and injustice based on class, 'race', gender and disability exist in playgroups, nurseries and schools, and that equal opportunities policies are not enough to ensure that staff look at their attitudes and feelings and act positively to work in partnership with parents.

A historical context is provided to explain how and why the concept of partnership with parents developed. Barriers deterring parental involvement are explored as are the particular problems for lone, black, minority ethnic, gay and lesbian, traveller and disabled parents. A checklist of approaches for overcoming barriers is provided.

Examples from practice include 'Travelling the anti-racist road with parents', mentioning work with parents – from readmission home visits to creative activities, and raising awareness as an ongoing team approach to work with children and their parents.

The final part 'Partnership for equality-theory into practice' introduces the background to the training exercises that focus on looking at workers' values, attitudes and practices so that they can confidently encourage parents to talk about their racist beliefs and to effectively challenge them. Thirteen training exercises, designed for use on initial and in-service training programmes include a number of typical scenarios: breaking the communication barrier; ensuring access; why don't they participate; and angry parents. Guidance suggests that these can be role played but trainers may want to use other approaches and prepare for managing groups where conflict is likely to arise so that this can be handled positively. There is a book and video list included.

The pack contains useful background information and exercises that contribute to filling 'the gap created by the failure of most traditional initial training courses'. Professionals in child development and parent education will find useful information and training approaches.

# A picture of health: breast screening

**FORMAT** Video pack: video, 15 min; booklet, 24-pages
**LANGUAGE** English
**AUDIENCE** Caribbean and African women
**PRICE** £35.00+VAT+p&p; £10.00+VAT+p&p (hire); free to organisations within the NHS Breast Screening Programme
**PRODUCER** London: Health First, Cultural Partnerships, 1994
**DISTRIBUTOR** Concord Video and Film Council, 201 Felixstowe Road, Ipswich IP3 9BJ. Tel: 01473 726012/715754; Fax: 01473 274531. Health First, Mary Sheridan House, 15 St Thomas' Street, London SE1 8RY. Tel: 020 7955 4366

This video, funded by the NHS Breast Screening Programme (NHSBSP) and the Department of Health, aims to inform Caribbean and African women about the importance of breast screening and the work of the NHSBSP. Although it specifically targets Caribbean and African women the issues are relevant to all women invited for breast screening (50–64 years). The video was developed in response to an identified need by an ethnic minorities and breast screening development worker.

The video begins with two women talking about their experiences of attending for breast screening and their feelings about it. This is followed by a short drama about a woman called Phyllis who receives a letter inviting her to attend for breast screening. She is disconcerted by the letter and discusses it with a friend. Phyllis identifies common worries women may have such as why has she been selected? Is something wrong? What might it find? Is it really necessary and how can she talk about it with her partner?

Her friend reassures her and recounts her own experience of attending for breast screening. Reluctantly, Phyllis talks with her husband about it. He is very supportive and attends the appointment with her. The visit to the screening centre and the actual procedure are shown in full – from checking-in with the receptionist through to confirming when the results will be available. Finally, Phyllis receives the results confirming that all is well. She is relieved and feels positive about the experience.

Throughout it is stressed that most women who are screened are found to be healthy and that early detection of breast cancer means treatment can be more effective. Key points, such as who is invited for screening, how to access the service, requesting an interpreter if needed, making convenient appointment times and that the service is free are continually re-enforced. The video has been made for group viewing and can be viewed as a whole or scene by scene. However, it is also suitable for individual viewing.

The accompanying teaching notes for presenters contains some background information about black women and breast cancer. They identify points for discussion with suggestions for planning group sessions and contain a scene by scene synopsis of the video. A short list of other resources relating to breast awareness and breast cancer is included.

This video was produced after consultations were held with local Caribbean and African women who requested that local women should be shown talking about their experiences. It can be used not only to inform women about breast screening but also to demonstrate best practice within the Breast Screening Programme; to raise awareness of the need to make services accessible to all; and of the anxieties a breast screening invitation may raise for women.

# Play and child development

**FORMAT** Video: 20 min; with some extra play ideas written (in English) inside the cover.
**LANGUAGE** Bengali, English, Gujarati, Hindi, Sylheti and Urdu
**AUDIENCE** Parents from black and minority ethnic groups and South Asian Communities, primary health care professional, community worker
**PRICE** £37.25 inc
**PRODUCER** Birmingham Council of British Pakistanis, 1995
**DISTRIBUTOR** N Films, 78 Holyhead Road, Handsworth, Birmingham B21 0LH. Tel: 0121 507 0341; Fax: 0121 554 1872

This bright, colourful video, presented to a background of South Asian music examines the importance of play, its educational value and how it enables child development. It was funded by the Department of Health.

It could be given to a parent or family to view alone or could be used by a health professional, or community worker to enable group work and discussion.

The video highlights traditional play, using artefacts from one's heritage, culture, folklore, story and song, as well as recognising and appreciating the world of play available in British culture.

The theme is building a relationship with children through play to give children confidence and security within their home and family environment. Whilst the whole family can be involved in playing with the child, the parent is encouraged to spend at least 10 minutes a day directly playing with their child in an encouraging and enjoyable way. The importance of praise is mentioned.

The video encourages talking in the parent's first language and reading stories from bilingual books. This enables a child to understand and develop speech, often in more than one language.

The importance of age appropriate toys is explained. An examination of household objects is made from a play perspective. The simplest of objects can be used to encourage creative play and stimulate imaginations. For example: cardboard boxes for creative play, building and storage; plastic and rubber objects for water play and bath time; wooden spoons, baking tins and saucepans for noisy play; and dressing up games – especially with friends.

Safety in the home is considered and a number of dangers are explained: fire; electrical sockets; medicines; and catches on cupboards.

Parents are encouraged to allow children of both genders to play at helping with cooking, cleaning and tidying, thus enabling them to gain concepts and grasp skills.

The video follows a family outing and suggestions are made about visits to enable children to explore the wider world; for example, visits to the park, local farm or zoo. Mother and toddler groups and playgroups are also suggested as these give the parent a chance to relax and meet others whilst allowing the child to extend their friendship circle and learn to play and mix. Advice is included on access to local play services.

# Pregnancy and childbirth

**FORMAT** Video, 49 min; script, 20-pages
**LANGUAGE** English
**AUDIENCE** Women
**PRICE** £52.50 inc.
**PRODUCER** Bristol: Refugee Action, 1997
**DISTRIBUTOR** Refugee Action, The Coach House, 2 Upper York Street, St Pauls, Bristol BS5 6AF. Tel: 0117 942 4613; Fax: 0117 944 1931

This video is for black and minority ethnic women who are thinking of having a baby, or who are pregnant or just had a baby. It was produced by Maternity and Health Links and Refugee Action in Bristol.

It is in four parts and covers all aspects of preparing for pregnancy, childbirth, antenatal care and caring for a new born baby at home. The video aims to give women as much information as possible about the services and entitlements they should receive. It features women, some with their partners, going through the different stages of ante- and postnatal care. For example, visiting the clinic, meeting the doctor, being examined and having a scan. The booklet is a transcript of the video.

This informative and accessible resource can be used by a facilitator with small groups of women to trigger discussion and questions.

# Promoting continence for women

**FORMAT** Video, 15 min
**LANGUAGE** Bengali, English, Punjabi (Mirpuri) and Urdu
**AUDIENCE** Women, continence advisors, primary health care teams

**PRICE** £12.50+p&p
**PRODUCER** Keighley: Continence Advisory Service, Airedale NHS Trust, 1995
**DISTRIBUTOR** The Continence Advisory Service, Keighley Health Centre, Oakworth Road, Keighley, West Yorkshire BD21 1SA. Tel: 01535 606111

This video aims to inform women about services and tips for managing incontinence and emphasises the importance of pelvic floor exercises as a means of preventing incontinence. It was produced by the Keighley Continence Advisory Service, Airedale NHS Trust.

The video, presented by a continence advisor, stresses that incontinence – leakage due to a loss of bladder or bowel control – is a common and treatable problem that can happen to anyone anytime. Most of the three million sufferers are women, who until recent campaigns to promote continence, felt that women were expected to live with incontinence. The triggers of incontinence – lifting, coughing, tea and coffee, and the causes such as the weakening of pelvic floor muscles during childbirth are mentioned.

The video shows women in a gym, an antenatal class and in a counselling session with a continence advisor, actively doing different things to improve their continence. Pelvic floor exercises are described in detail and these are recommended both during and after pregnancy. Special products for continence management are referred to as available from a continence advisor. The Urdu, Bengali and Punjabi versions are presented by continence advisors from the relevant communities.

A consultant urologist confirms that incontinence is widespread and treatable, and that early treatment is recommended.

An encouraging account is presented by an older woman describing her experience of regaining complete continence after a lifetime of incontinence.

This video is positive, practical and encouraging. It would be useful as a trigger for group discussions, for women to view at home and with ante- and postnatal groups. It can be used to support advice from health professionals.

# Racial equality means business: a standard for racial quality for employers

**FORMAT** Pack: A4, spiral bound paperback, 56-pages
**LANGUAGE** English
**AUDIENCE** Employers, occupational health workers, human resource departments
**PRICE** £10.00+10%p&p
**PRODUCER** London: Commission for Racial Equality, 1995
**DISTRIBUTOR** Central Books, 99 Wallis Road, London E9 5LN. Tel: 020 8986 5488; Fax: 020 8533 5821; e-mail: peter@centbks.demon.co.uk

This book was designed to help employers set a standard for developing racial equality strategies and to measure their impact. It covers employment issues and activities undertaken as 'corporate citizens'.
The pack could be used by the human resources department or company directors/managers, as well as equal opportunities trainers/facilitators.

The book is divided into five sections. Section 1 is an introduction to the Commission for Racial Equality (CRE). It defines the CRE standard, who can use it and outlines the following four sections. It links the standard to related initiatives, and demonstrates how to use the standard flexibly for assessment, development and growth and outcomes. This section also highlights the checklist and measurements of progress.

Section 2, 'The Case for Action', examines the business case. In particular, it covers: using people's talents to the full; ensuring that selection decisions and policies are based on objective criteria, and not on unlawful discrimination, prejudice or unfair assumption; and becoming an employer of choice. The latter includes understanding customers' needs, operating internationally with success, sustaining a healthy society, making the company more attractive to investors, customers and clients, and avoiding the costs of discrimination.

Section 3 is a checklist that summarises the range of action involved in considering, planning and implementing a racial equality programme. This would involve commitment, action and outcomes.

In section 4, 'Measurements', there are fold-out charts for six areas. These show at a glance the requirements at each of five progressive levels. The six areas include:
- area 1 – policy and planning;
- area 2 – selection;
- area 3 – developing and retaining staff;
- area 4 – communication and corporate image;
- area 5 – corporate citizenship;
- area 6 – auditing for racial equality quality.

The final section contains three appendices: a glossary of terms; a list of useful publications; and a list of useful organisations.

# Reaching people – guidelines for the development and evaluation of sexual health materials in a multiracial society

**FORMAT** Pack, 50-pages
**LANGUAGE** English
**AUDIENCE** Sexual health workers
**PRICE** £10.55 inc.
**PRODUCER** Birmingham: Aquarius Action Projects, 1996
**DISTRIBUTOR** Aquarius ETC, 6th Floor, The White House, 111 New Street, Birmingham B2 4EU. Tel: 0121 632 4727; Fax: 0121 633 0539
**ISBN** 0952859904

This report for health professionals was the result of a project commissioned by West Midlands Regional Health Authority/Regional Office and managed by Aquarius ETC. The aim of the report is to complete a review of sexual health education materials designed for use with black and minority ethnic groups. It is a useful resource for professionals involved in the process of reviewing and developing health-related resources.

The report raises awareness about the appropriateness of resources for the targeted groups and highlights the need for them to be accessible and free from discrimination and bias. It also raises a number of issues about the inconsistency of reviews and good practice.

The report is in three parts: setting the agenda; the development process; and the evaluation questionnaire. It contains a useful glossary of some commonly used terms. The content includes appropriate formats, translation, text, imagery and consultation.

This is a practical working document for assessing and cataloguing sexual health resources. The comprehensive questionnaire provided is one method of doing this and there are good practice guidelines for developing future resources.

# Religion, ethnicity and sex education: exploring the issues

**FORMAT** Pack, 124-pages
**LANGUAGE** English
**AUDIENCE** Teachers, lecturers, parents, trainers
**PRICE** £10.50 (Bureau members), £15.50 (non-members)
**PRODUCER** London: National Children's Bureau, 1993
**DISTRIBUTOR** National Children's Bureau, 8 Wakley Street, London EC1V 7QE. Tel: 020 7843 6000

This resource is for teachers and others working with young people. It aims to enable them to grasp the range of religious and moral perspectives on sexuality and personal relationships, so that they are able to respond to the needs and identities of the young people with whom they work. It was produced by the National Children's Bureau for the Sex Education Forum, an umbrella group of 30 religious and secular organisations concerned with provision and support of sex education for young people.

The pack is the result of a project on religion and ethnicity undertaken by the Sex Education Forum. A questionnaire was sent to representatives of seven religious groups. The responses form the bulk of the resource and cover the broader philosophy and rationale behind specific religious prescriptions, plus views on sexuality and sex education. The wide diversity of opinion and belief within each religion is stressed and each response should not be considered an authoritative religious perspective. Responses cover Anglican, Hindu, Islamic, Jewish, Methodist, Roman Catholic and Sikh perspectives plus a secular perspective. A personal story about a young Asian Muslim man who is gay is also included. There is a section on equal opportunities and sex education with a checklist for teachers.

The pack will be of interest to all teachers concerned with sex education and should enable them to plan such work more effectively and consult with parents and communities more confidently. It includes some activities that can be used in inset training or at parents' and staff meetings to open up discussion about this sensitive subject. They are quite challenging and probably need an experienced facilitator. The relevant requirements of the National Curriculum are noted and there is a reading list of other helpful resources. A range of people from different communities who are experienced in personal and health education contributed to the development of the resource.

## Rishtae aur zimmevarian: relationships and responsibilities: sexual health programme with black and minority ethnic communities: a training pack and report

**FORMAT** Pack: 100-pages, A4 resources sheets x 30; report, 150-pages
**LANGUAGE** English
**AUDIENCE** Trainers, facilitators, youth and community workers, sexual health and other health care workers
**AUTHOR(S)** A. Robin, G. Singh and H. Thompson (eds.)
**PRICE** £35.00+£4.50p&p pack and report); £25.00+£3.00p&p (pack only); £15.00+£3.00p&p (report only)

**PRODUCER** Preston: North West Lancashire Health Promotion Unit, 1995
**DISTRIBUTOR** North West Lancashire Health Promotion Unit, Sharoe Green Hospital, Sharoe Green Lane, Fulwood, Preston, Lancashire PR2 8DU.
Tel: 01772 711772; Fax: 01772 711113
**ISBN** 1900596008

This training pack is for facilitators, trainers, youth and community workers, and sexual and other health professionals who work with people from black and minority ethnic groups. Users need community work experience and some knowledge of HIV/AIDS and sexual health issues.

The pack outlines a framework of training interventions to use with groups of people from different faiths and cultures. It describes eleven schemes that took place in Preston. Some of these could be replicated elsewhere but others would need adapting, additional resources or considerable preparatory work.

The pack includes resource sheets for the programme activities – questionnaires, quizzes, exercises, scenarios, and reference sheets. Additional background materials, particularly on HIV/AIDS and sexual health, may sometimes be needed, both for course participants and trainers. A list of organisations that supply literature on this topic is provided but no reading list for trainers.

The interventions that can be used as presented are a two-day residential 'train the trainers' programme, and residential weekend courses for Hindu men, Muslim boys, young professional Muslim men and young Sikh men. Two seminar days that would need adapting are also included, one looking at sex education in schools from a Hindu perspective, and the other focusing on the production of a sex education leaflet for black and minority ethnic parents. Those interventions that are covered only in outline are training sessions for young Muslim mothers, Muslim girls, Hindu and Muslim women, and older women.

The pack also explains training and facilitation techniques and includes evaluation sheets and ideas for preparatory group work.

North West Lancashire Health Promotion Unit developed the pack after undertaking action research and needs assessment. This indicated that much HIV/AIDS and sexual health material is not relevant to black and minority ethnic groups in Preston.

# Safe: a video resource for work with young men

**FORMAT** Video pack: video, 25 min, colour; booklet, 17-pages
**LANGUAGE** English
**AUDIENCE** 14–19-year-olds, Key Stage 4
**PRICE** £39.95 inc.
**PRODUCER** London: The Young Men's Video Project, 1995
**DISTRIBUTOR** The B Team (Resources for Boys Work), 320 Commercial Way, London SE15 1QN. Tel/Fax: 020 7732 9409

This video pack aims to raise issues and develop work with young people, especially young black men, around the themes of health, homophobia, masculinity, race, relationships, sex and responsibility.

The pack consists of a video and booklet. The video employs drama to tell a story in 16 scenes using actors. The storyline hinges around the relationships of four young Black and South Asian men who live together in the house of one of their parents. Characterisation and motivation are complex, raising several issues for

discussion. For example, Delroy, a young black man has insulin dependent diabetes. His possession of injecting equipment and a mobile phone leads another young man's girlfriend, whom Delroy has taunted with sexist comments, to assume he is using and dealing with heroin.

The booklet provides a short introduction and background to the video programme with ideas for use. One section provides a breakdown of how the various themes are raised throughout the video. Another section examines the facts and fiction associated with the young men's attitudes and behaviour shown in the video. These can be used by facilitators to highlight key issues for discussion and learning points.

The pack uses participatory methods, including group discussion and decision making, and requires basic facilitation skills. The pack is not prescriptive about the methods but encourages users to consider a variety of ways of using the pack as a catalyst to discuss issues with young men. It advises that different outcomes may result depending upon whether the group is predominantly white, or black, or single gender or mixed.

This resource can be used in schools, colleges and youth and community settings.

The video addresses a wide range of issues around race, gender, sexuality and popular conceptions of drug and alcohol use. The accompanying booklet highlights where these issues are raised in the programme and includes a list of fact/fiction points to counter stereotypes. The narrative and issues raised in the video depend on visual clues as well as verbal and this may restrict its use for blind and partially sighted young people.

The pack was funded by West Midlands Regional Health Authority, Birmingham City Challenge, Birmingham Leisure and Community Services and North Birmingham Community Trust. An evaluation sheet is included with the pack and feedback on the use of the video is encouraged.

# Safely home?

**FORMAT** Video 30 min; booklet, 26-pages, illustrated
**LANGUAGES** Bengali/English and Urdu/English
**AUDIENCE** Parents and carers
**PRICE** £29.50 inc.
**PRODUCER** Bradford: Safely Home Project, 1993
**DISTRIBUTOR** Safely Home, c/o Jean Wilson, Manningham Health Centre, Lumb Lane, Bradford BD8 7SY.
Tel: 01274 724298; Fax: 01274 774880

This video aims to raise awareness about accident prevention in the home and can be used to trigger discussion and inform parents and carers. The video was produced by the Safely Home Project and funded by the Bradford Community Trust. It is primarily available in English with Bengali and Urdu voice-overs.

The video focuses on Sabiha, an Asian girl, who sustains serious burns from an unguarded fire and is facially disfigured. Her mother is interviewed in her home with a translator. She explains how the accident happened and the consequences for Sabiha in terms of hospitalisation and treatment. The video also highlights other 'trouble spots' in the home such as unguarded stairs and ironing on the floor, and how they can be avoided.

Some parts of the video include scenes that may cause the viewer to make assumptions about other cultures as there is no explanation for their inclusion. For example, a white girl is seen playing with toys in front of a guarded fire. The facilitator should be aware of this and feel able to deal with any issues arising from the video.

The accompanying booklet has no text and could be confusing. On one side of each double-page spread are colour pictures of children injured through accidents in the home, with advice about what to do on the opposite page, for example run water on a burn, or call for an ambulance. There are also pictures of accidents about to happen and drawings of how they might be prevented but these may need clarification.

There are no notes or guidance on how to use this video and booklet, so careful preparation is needed. Facilitators might find other accident prevention material suitable for use to support this resource. It could be used in various settings but would probably suit work with individuals or with small groups.

# Schizophrenia: notes for relatives and friends
# Psychiatric diagnosis: notes for relatives and patients

**FORMAT** Pack: Booklets, 8-pages and 4-pages
**LANGUAGE** Bengali, English, Punjabi and Urdu
**AUDIENCE** Carers, mental health teams, primary health care teams, general public
**PRICE** Free
**PRODUCER** West Bromwich: National Schizophrenia Fellowship, 1994
**DISTRIBUTOR** National Schizophrenia Fellowship, Midlands Regional Office, 9 St Michael's Court, Victoria Street, West Bromwich B70 8EZ. Tel: 0121 500 5988

The main eight-page booklet in the pack is for relatives and friends of people diagnosed as having schizophrenia. It describes the symptoms, causes and treatment and what can be done to help those with schizophrenia. It was written by psychiatrists.

The booklet describes in depth how a person with schizophrenia may behave and how they may seem to people who know them well. Some of the believed causes of schizophrenia and contributory factors such as stress are discussed. Treatment is generally explained and it is emphasised that it must be continued even when a person feels they are well or recovered. Advice is given about how to support a person with schizophrenia. The booklet does not deal with the controversial opinions that surround diagnosis of schizophrenia. The English version includes addresses for the National Schizophrenia Fellowship around the country but the other language versions do not and people may need to be given this information. This is an informative booklet that may help people to understand more about schizophrenia.

The accompanying four-page booklet seeks to explain how mental health professionals come to make a diagnosis and why a diagnosis may sometimes change. It is densely typed and is only available in English. Issues involved in making a diagnosis when the health professional and patient do not share a common language or culture are not discussed.

## Sickle cell anaemia

**FORMAT** Booklet, 26-pages
**LANGUAGE** English
**AUDIENCE** Health care professionals, primary health care teams, commissioners, service providers

**PRICE** Free
**PRODUCER** Leeds: NHS Management Executive, 1993
**DISTRIBUTOR** Department of Health Distribution Centre, PO Box 410, Wetherby, West Yorkshire LS23 7LN. Tel: 01937 840250; Fax: 01937 845381

This booklet for health care purchasers may also be of interest to providers and users of services. It addresses health services for people with sickle cell disorders. Part of a series produced by the NHSME the booklet aims to present users' views about current services and about what they think makes up a quality service. The booklet was prepared with help from the Sickle Cell Society, people affected by sickle cell disorders and a lecturer in community genetic counselling.

The booklet briefly outlines what sickle cell anaemia is, its causes, symptoms and treatments. The responses of primary and acute health care services are outlined with suggestions for good practice. Difficulties that users experience with these services are noted.

Emphasis is placed on the role that specialist nurses can play, plus the importance of advocates for some users. Throughout, the booklet quotes from service users who highlight various issues, especially the severity of pain during a crisis and the need for speedy pain relief. They particularly note the difficulties in persuading health professionals of the severity of their pain and the need for speedy pain relief. It is stressed that sickle cell can be a very serious and painful disorder. A checklist is included to assist purchasers in examining how well their services are meeting the needs of people with sickle cell disorders.

This booklet is short enough to be read by everyone who may purchase or provide services for people with sickle cell disorders. It provides a useful basis for discussion about services and strongly states users' points of view.

## Sickle cell anaemia and thalassaemia teaching pack

**FORMAT** Pack, 32-pages, A4 OHPs x 32 colour
**LANGUAGE** English
**AUDIENCE** Health care professionals, people with sickle cell anaemia and their families
**PRICE** £53.00
**PRODUCER** Luton: South Bedfordshire Community Health Care Trust, 1996
**DISTRIBUTOR** South Bedfordshire Community Health Care Trust, 1 Union Street, Luton, Bedfordshire LU1 3AN. Tel: 01582 485888; Fax: 01582 485667

This teaching pack is aimed at health professionals and allied professions. It aims to help health professionals make informed decisions about medical and nursing care and to advise those with sickle cell anaemia, their families and the general public. Although primarily for those in contact with people who have sickle cell anaemia and thalassaemia, it can be used with other professionals such as police officers and teachers.

The pack is in three parts: introduction and training pack guidelines; the training pack and notes; and a set of overheads for use in the delivery of the course. It is designed for use in the form of a lecture, training session or workshop. Some of the sessions can be used independently of each other and last between one hour to half a day, depending on the level of participants' knowledge. Notes for the trainer accompany each section with guidelines on how to manage the session.

The pack covers all the medical aspects of the disorder including sessions on the physiology of the blood, diagnosis of sickle cell and thalassaemia, types of crisis and genetic inheritance and carriers. Participants may not be familiar with some of the medical terms used so a glossary would be a useful additional handout. The material is detailed and the trainer will need to have a basic knowledge of the subject and have studied the course in order to facilitate the session effectively.

## Sigarayi birak yasamaya bak

*See* Give up smoking for the good life

## The smoke inside us

**VARIANT TITLE** Icimizdeki duman
**FORMAT** Video, 19 min
**LANGUAGE** Turkish (with and without English subtitles)
**AUDIENCE** Turkish people, particularly smokers
**PRICE** £38.00 inc.
**PRODUCER** London: East London and The City Health Promotion, 1994
**DISTRIBUTOR** Commercial Relations and Health Promotion, East London and The City Health Authority, Aneurin Bevan House, 81–91 Commerical Road, London E1 1RD. Tel: 020 7655 6600; Fax: 020 7655 6666

This video aims to raise awareness and provide information about smoking – why people smoke, what it costs, how smoking affects the smoker and other people, particularly in terms of their health. It explores local Turkish people's attitudes and beliefs about smoking.

It is filmed in a documentary style, featuring the Turkish-speaking community in Haringey and Hackney in their daily lives. The video explores their attitudes and beliefs about smoking, including the views of children and young people, as well as older men and women. It is estimated that three-quarters of the men and half the women in this community smoke.

It is organised under five main headings: the cost of smoking; smoking and young people; effects on your health; smoking and pregnancy; and passive smoking. Each section features the opinions of local people and highlights key facts and figures. There are interviews with health and community professionals. Health issues such as how smoking causes narrowing of the arteries are explained. However, there is also a harrowing scene with cancer patients in Haseki Hospital, Istanbul. It is questionable whether seeing such scenes will influence smokers to stop.

The video is addressed to the smoker and could be viewed at home. It might also be useful to health and community workers as a trigger for a discussion on smoking, although there are no accompanying notes. The video suggests that those who want help to stop smoking should watch the video *Give up smoking for the good life*, or contact their local health centre. Many local organisations are acknowledged for their support in making the video, which was produced with additional funding from Europe Against Cancer.

# Speaking out

**FORMAT** Book, 221-pages
**LANGUAGE** English
**AUDIENCE** Women, black and minority ethnic women, trainers, youth and community workers, health promotion
**AUTHORS** R. Martin and C. Whitehead
**PRICE** £14.99
**PRODUCER** London: Health Education Authority, 1994

**DISTRIBUTOR** HEA Customer Services, Marston Book Services, P O Box 269, Abingdon, Oxon OX14 4YN.
Tel: 01235 465565; Fax: 01235 465556

A well thought out, easy to use book that will be of interest to assertiveness trainers, facilitators, youth workers, community workers, education tutors, health promotion workers and outreach workers working with women. It shows women how to plan, adapt and run courses for groups. The book contains a variety of discussion and activity exercises. Throughout the book all photocopiable handouts are individually marked.

There is a separate section of exercises for women from black and minority ethnic communities.

It is divided into five main sections. Section 1, 'Planning and facilitating', provides a basic overview of how to work with groups and the issues to consider. For example: different types of groups; practical arrangements; setting aims and objectives; ground rules; equal opportunities; potential problems; and evaluation.

The second section, 'Frameworks', discusses meeting the needs of the group and offers suggestions for putting exercises together to develop sessions/courses.

Sections three and four contain a variety of exercises. Each activity is clearly laid out with subheadings about the aims, who it is for, materials required, the method, discussion and issues raised.

The activities in 'Exercise Section I' are general exercises on assertiveness and health with themed subsections: Self-esteem and confidence; how we talk to ourselves; how we see ourselves; communicating with others; health and sexual health; rights and responsibilities; anger; and dealing with criticism.

The exercises in 'Exercise Section II' are specifically for black and minority ethnic women. The term 'black' is used to describe women from black and minority ethnic communities as it was the term preferred as affirming by women developing this resource. This section contains many discussion-based exercises and covers: taking part; ground rules; working together; assertiveness and our own health; speaking out: weighing up the costs to health; counteracting the stresses in our lives; case studies: supporting others; and activities to promote self-esteem and well-being.

The final 'Resources' section is a list divided into three parts: planning and facilitating; for all women's groups; and for black women's groups.

# Starting your baby on solid foods

**FORMAT** Video 15 min x 2
**LANGUAGE** Bengali with English subtitles
**AUDIENCE** Parents
**PRICE** £30.00 inc. (purchase); £10.00 (3-day preview)
**PRODUCER** London: East London and The City Health Promotion, 1994
**DISTRIBUTOR** Commercial Relations and Health Promotion, East London and The City Health Authority, Aneurin Bevan House, 81–91 Commercial Road, London E1 1RD. Tel: 020 7655 6600; Fax: 020 7655 6666

This video aims to provide advice, information and encouragement for the introduction of Asian foods into a baby's diet as part of the weaning process. The importance of a healthy diet is stressed throughout and babies of varying ages are seen enjoying a range of foods independently, with their mothers and families. This video was produced by East London and the City Health in conjunction with the maternity services liaison scheme.

It offers practical tips on selecting, preparing and feeding traditional Asian family foods to babies. The information is presented in stages, covering the baby's dietary needs from birth to 12 months. Throughout a voice-over commentary accompanies displays of different types of fresh and cooked foods. Brand named products are included with advice on checking sell-by dates, selecting 'no added sugar' products and avoiding sweetened foods. Manufactured vegetarian baby foods are recommended as suitable for halal diets. We see some foods being prepared, leaving out chili, salt and sugar. Good hygiene practices are demonstrated such as sterilising plastic utensils in the microwave.

The importance of supervising baby's eating and including the baby in meals with the family is stressed. The video ends with a summary of the main points. Users of the video should note that eggs and carrots are mentioned and that advice about feeding these to babies have changed.

This informative and encouraging video could be used as a discussion trigger for parents and carers discussing their experiences of introducing family foods into their babies diets. The distinct phases allow the video to be used selectively. It would be of benefit to all parents wanting to introduce their baby to a wider range of foods at an early stage.

# Stroke: questions and answers

**FORMAT** Booklet, 12-pages

**LANGUAGE** Bengali, Chinese, English, Gujarati, Hindi, Punjabi and Urdu
**AUDIENCE** Stroke patients, carers and families of stroke patients
**PRICE** Free (single copies)
**PRODUCER** London: The Stroke Association, 1994
**DISTRIBUTOR** The Stroke Association, Administration Department, Charles House, 61–69 Derngate, Northampton NN1 1UE. Tel: 01604 231000; Fax: 01604 697137

The booklet aims to provide answers to some general questions about stroke: what a stroke is; the after-effects; treatment; rehabilitation; and resources available for patients and carers. It is intended for patients who have had a stroke, their families and carers.

A question and answer format is used throughout to describe the causes, symptoms and after effects of stroke on the heart, brain, vision, speech and movement. Information given covers risks of a second stroke, recovery rates, hospitalisation, medical treatments, rehabilitation, regaining independence, aggression, sexual relationships, support for and from relatives and state benefits.

The booklet recognises the emotional stresses of the stroke patient and their relatives and recommends expressing these views to others in support groups and/or with appropriate professionals. This clearly presented resource will enable people who have had a stroke and their carers to get practical information and support. It includes a comprehensive reference list and suggestions for further reading, resources and organisations. For example, SPOD is recommended for people with disabilities who want support with personal sexual difficulties.

Information about financial support from social security predates recent changes in social security policy and readers will need to seek current advice. The final part of the booklet lists Stroke Association services and publications.

# Take care of your heart

**FORMAT** Audio-cassette, 14 min.
**LANGUAGE** Bangladeshi (Sylheti dialect) with English translation of script
**AUDIENCE** Bangladeshi (Sylheti speaking) groups
**PRICE** £3.00
**PRODUCER** London: Culture Waves for Camden & Islington Health Promotion, 1994
**DISTRIBUTOR** Camden & Islington Health Promotion, St Pancras Hospital, 4 St Pancras Way, London NW1 0PE. Tel: 020 7530 3900; Fax: 020 7530 3922

This audio-cassette drama concentrates on the prevention of coronary heart disease. It could be used by health professionals and link workers to promote relevant discussion, either with individuals or perhaps with a community group.

The drama centres on Lukman, a family man in his 40s. He has just returned from the funeral of a friend who died from a heart attack. Lukman feels upset but his mother advises him that whatever happens is the will of Allah and that young people should not worry. However, Sufia, Lukman's wife feels he should be proactive and consult their GP. Lukman believes that women do not suffer from heart disease.

The doctor examines Lukman and discovers a pulled muscle. He then goes on to explain that that there is a high rate of heart disease in the Bengali community, including women. Sufia and Lukman's mother are also examined. All have blood pressure checks and discuss diabetes.

The doctor explains that a change of lifestyle can help reduce the risk of heart disease and that regular blood pressure checks are important. The lifestyle changes covered include: more exercise; weight loss, and diet, particularly the need to reduce salt and fat and increase the consumption of fresh fruit and vegetables. The traditional diet is examined and the family are given advice, including where to go for further help.

The doctor explains the health risks associated with smoking and Lukman says he will try to stop smoking.

The benefits of exercise for people of all ages are highlighted, including stress reduction. The advice about aerobic exercise (20 minutes, two to three times per week) should be updated in line with the current Department of Health recommendation for 30 minutes, five times per week.

Facilitators using this audio-cassette may need to supplement the information with details of local support and help – for example, stop smoking groups or local leisure and community centres.

# Talking about miscarriage

**FORMAT** Audio-cassette; 12 min 30 seconds; notes, 8-pages in various languages with English translation
**LANGUAGE** English, also available in Bangla (Sylehti), Mirpuri and Urdu
**AUDIENCE** Women from black and minority ethnic groups; support groups
**PRICE** £1.75
**PRODUCER** Wakefield: The Miscarriage Association, 1997

**DISTRIBUTOR** Miscarriage Association, Clayton Hospital, Northgate, Wakefield, West Yorkshire WF1 3JS.
Tel: 01924 200 799; Fax: 01924 298 834

This audio-cassette is intended for women who have had a miscarriage. It aims to explain the reasons for miscarriage and to offer support and help in dealing with the emotional and physical effects. Women could listen to the cassette on their own as they are encouraged to seek help. It could also be used in a supported environment, either in a one-to-one situation or in a group, so that women have the opportunity to ask questions and share their feelings.

The cassette contains a play in which a young woman who has recently miscarried gets support and information from a doctor and a friend. The listener learns that miscarriages are common, with approximately one in four pregnancies ending in miscarriage. The reasons given include:
● often because there is something wrong with the foetus and it is nature's way of not continuing a pregnancy that won't turn out right;
● sometimes because of hormone problems;
● possibly the shape or lining of the womb has an effect on the pregnancy;
● possibly because of an infection.

The cassette explores women's feelings of guilt and the fears they experience, including feeling ashamed and wanting to keep the miscarriage a secret. Further support from the Miscarriage Association is explained, including the importance of talking to someone who understands, either by contacting a local volunteer, or a support group.

The short leaflet, written by women who have had miscarriages, associates with the reader's loss and empathises with her feelings. Through a series of questions and answers the booklet discusses the mixture of emotions women may feel and various strategies for coping with them. This can include turning to your 'husband' and family, and remembering the baby you have lost and saying goodbye.

The leaflet covers health issues and explains why an operation (a D & C) may have been necessary, as well as bleeding, bathing and showering, periods, and becoming pregnant again. The causes of miscarriage, looking to the future, and sources of help and support are covered.

# Teeth for life

**FORMAT** Video pack: videos x 2, 13 min and 19 min; trainers' guide, 95-pages
**LANGUAGE** Bengali, Punjabi or Urdu with English subtitles
**AUDIENCE** General public, health professionals
**PRICE** £20.00+VAT+p&p
**PRODUCER** London: Health Education Authority, 1993
**DISTRIBUTOR** Concord Film and Video Council, 201 Felixstowe Road, Ipswich IP3 9BJ. Tel: 01473 726012

This trigger video pack is for health professionals and lay workers and aims to help them promote oral/dental health education among Asian communities. It consists of a video in two parts and an accompanying booklet of notes for trainers. The pack was developed as a response to research findings about Asian communities' experiences of dental health services. It was developed by the Health Education Authority with joint funding from the Department of Health. Drama is used to explore issues about oral health.

Part one opens with a family returning from a party. The children brush their teeth properly, but their parents have some problems that lead to them making appointments with the dentist. In part two the parents visit the dentist for the first time. Anxieties people may have about dental visits are addressed and what to expect during a visit is covered. Animated sequences are used to explain gingivitis and periodontal disease. Photographs of various dental treatments 'before and after' are shown.

The booklet for trainers covers aims, objectives and points to consider when planning sessions. There are 13 suggested sessions covering a range of issues, which can be used flexibly according to time available and audience interest. The pack has been designed for use by a wide range of people and the booklet notes that only two of the sessions would need the involvement of a health professional. The pack does not deal with dental decay or diet related to dental health and suggests other resources can be used to deal with these topics.

This pack is unusual because it deals with topics not often addressed, such as anxieties about going to the dentist and worries about cost. Sessions are designed to encourage informed discussion and to take account of people's religious, cultural and spiritual values. For example, one session suggests points for discussion for a Muslim audience about dental treatment during Ramadan. Although designed for use in a group setting there may be occasions when it is appropriate for home viewing by individuals, perhaps with a health professional (for example, to reassure someone about what to expect at the dentist). Each language version of the video has been filmed separately with different actors so that dress and names, for example, reflect the cultural group more accurately. The pack was developed in consultation with members of Asian communities.

## Travel and diabetes

*See* Driving with Diabetes

## Travelling people

**FORMAT** Video, 50 min
**LANGUAGE** English
**AUDIENCE** Travellers, community workers, health professionals, service providers, primary health care teams
**PRICE** £25.00 inc.
**PRODUCER** Northern Visions, 1993
**DISTRIBUTOR** Northern Visions, 4 Donegall Street Place, Belfast BT1 2FN. Tel: 01232 245495; Fax: 01232 326608

This documentary explores the experiences of travelling people in Ireland, their culture, language and way of life and the discrimination they face daily. It was made by Northern Visions in close cooperation with traveller activists and the Dublin Travellers Education Development Group.

Throughout the video travellers emphasise that they see themselves as an ethnic group and that discrimination against travellers is racism. Covert filming shows travellers being refused a drink in a pub and being verbally abused. Interviews with people in the street reflect prejudice and ignorance. Health, housing, education and politics are all explored from travellers' experiences. The lack of services and adequate sites for caravans is documented and stereotypes of travellers challenged. Although the video describes the situation in Ireland it is also relevant to Britain and gives travellers a voice. The video ends with scenes of a unique housing development that has been developed by a local authority in consultation with the traveller community it will house.

The video is suitable for general viewing by any group. It may be appropriate for service providers in raising awareness about traveller communities and meeting the needs of all sections of the community. It could also be used with traveller groups to explore how to gain access to services and challenge inequality.

## Weaning

**FORMAT** Video, 30 min
**LANGUAGE** Bengali, English, Gujarati, Hindi/Urdu and Punjabi
**AUDIENCE** Women
**PRICE** £37.25 inc.
**PRODUCER** Birmingham: N Films, 1995
**DISTRIBUTOR** N Films Ltd, 78 Holyhead Road, Handsworth, Birmingham B21 0LH. Tel: 0121 507 0341; Fax: 0121 554 1872

The video aims to give parents information about weaning babies. The film is set mainly in a health centre where an Asian health visitor is giving a talk to Asian mothers, inviting their questions and providing answers. A narrator translates the key points that are raised.

The talk is divided into sections to explore the three stages of weaning; four to six months, six to nine months and nine months to a year. At each stage, advice and information is given about the signs to look for to see if a baby is ready for the relevant stage of weaning, the sorts of food that can be introduced, how the food can be prepared and the implements that can be used for feeding.

The video covers common questions and concerns about weaning. It emphasises the 'dos' and 'don'ts' of ensuring that babies have a healthy and balanced diet. The film shows different meals being prepared which are appropriate for babies of different ages. At the end of each section a suggested daily menu is presented as a written summary.

The children and mothers featured in the film are participants at a talk at Leicester Asian Ladies Circle. The video does not show any men feeding babies or cooking. There are no disabled parents or children featured. The video includes information about foods from Asian and English cultures. It also includes advice on how to give a vegetarian baby a healthy and balanced diet when weaning.

The video gives advice about who to ask for further information or help and at the end of the film the key tips are summarised.

The resource could be used by parents in their own homes, by health visitors as a way of discussing the topic and by health education centres or community centres working with new parents. As the video focuses mainly on food from Asian cultures, a facilitator using it as part of an information or training session would need knowledge of nutrition and foods from diverse cultures.

The video was produced by the Department of Health with the Leicester Asian Ladies Circle. It does not state how it was developed or whether it was piloted, but a large advisory panel is credited in the titles.

# Weaning your baby

**VARIANT TITLE** Ababinta Ilmahaaga
**FORMAT** Audio-cassette, 16 min
**LANGUAGE** Somali (one side of tape) and English (other side of tape)

**AUDIENCE** Somali speaking parents, Black and minority ethnic groups
**PRICE** £5.00 (inclusive)
**PRODUCER** London: East London and City Health Promotion,1997
**DISTRIBUTOR** Commercial Relations and Health Promotion, East London and The City Health Authority, Aneurin Bevan House, 81–91 Commercial Road, London E1 1RD. Tel: 020 7655 6600; Fax: 020 7655 6666

This audio-cassette is aimed at Somali-speaking parents. It suggests appropriate meals and drinks for babies at each stage of their development during the first 12 months of life. It could be used by health visitors or other members of the primary health care team and link workers, and would probably work best if listened to with a group of parents and then discussed afterwards.

The first half of the cassette advises on the preparation of healthy food. The second half suggests which meals a baby can eat after four, six, nine, and 12 months. The importance of breast feeding during the first four months of a baby's life is explained at the start, although there is recognition of the fact that some women will need to bottle feed. Parents are reassured that their baby will get all the nourishment needed this way.

There are many tips on food safety, including the storage of made-up baby food, not adding flavours, particularly sugars, salt and spices, heating and re-heating baby foods and sterilisation of baby equipment and work surfaces.

There are ideas to encourage baby to eat and to make meal times enjoyable, for example:
● allow the baby to see what's happening;
● go at the baby's own pace;
● never force a baby to eat;

- provide a flat plastic spoon and plastic bowl and feeder cup to encourage baby to feed;
- give the baby food it can pick up with its fingers;
- never leave a baby unattended whilst it is eating or drinking.

Parents are urged to contact their health visitor or Somali link worker if they have any concerns.

# What is thalassaemia?

**FORMAT** Pack, 117-pages, tables, illustrated
**LANGUAGE** English
**AUDIENCE** People with thalassaemia, primary health care teams
**AUTHORS** R. Vullo, B. Modell and E. Georganda
**PRICE** £1.00 inc.
**PRODUCER** Cyprus: Thalassaemia International Federation, 1995
**DISTRIBUTOR** UK Thalassaemia Society, 107 Nightingale Lane, London N8 7QY. Tel: 020 8348 0437

This book aims to explain the inherited disease of thalassaemia, its effects, treatment and expectations for future developments in managing and treating the disease. The target audience includes doctors, nurses, parents of thalassaemic children and adults with thalassaemia. The book was written by doctors and is printed and distributed by the Thalassaemia International Federation with the co-operation of The World Health Organization.

The book is divided into four sections: introduction to thalassaemia; thalassaemia major; other types of beta-thalassaemia; and psychological aspects of thalassaemia. The back of the book contains pro-forma charts for keeping records

about thalassaemia patients as well as a list of addresses of thalassaemia associations worldwide.

The information is presented in the form of questions and answers. In the introduction, for example, the main questions addressed are: 'What is thalassaemia?' and 'How is it inherited?' These questions are then sub-divided into further questions such as: 'What is blood?'; 'What is blood made of?'; 'What does blood do?'; 'What is anaemia?'; 'How do you measure anaemia?'; and 'How is thalassaemia passed on from parents to their children?'. The answers are provided through text, diagrams, charts and photographs. In places, the information is necessarily complex and medically technical, but the writers attempt to present it in an accessible way.

Section two, 'Thalassaemia major', covers the following areas in detail: the effects of the disease; blood transfusion; the spleen and splenectomy; bone-marrow transplantation; iron overload and Desferal; Desferal and the pump; other problems in thalassaemia; puberty; HIV/AIDS; and questions about the future.

Section three gives information about thalassaemia intermedia, its particular problems and thalassaemia associated with an 'abnormal haemoglobin'.

The fourth section explains the pychological aspects of the disease. It presents and discusses the common anxieties of parents and patients. For example, the emotional impact that having a child with the disease can have on other family members, and strategies for managing, as well as getting appropriate support for the whole family. This section also explores the development of the child who has thalassaemia using Erik Erikson's model of the eight stages of life. Again, ways of supporting the child to grow pyschologically through each stage are suggested. Questions such as 'Can I be open about myself and not get hurt?' and 'What kind of work should I consider?' are discussed, with the emphasis on living life to the full without ignoring the impact of coping with the disease.

The book does not explore issues around ethnicity, culture, gender or class. Readers are invited to write to the authors about the content, particularly where it is unclear or upsetting. It also asks for readers views and experiences so that these can be included in future editions. This text is the second edition.

# While you are pregnant: how to avoid infection from food and from contact with animals

**FORMAT** Booklet, 11-pages
**LANGUAGE** Bengali, Chinese, English, Greek, Gujarati, Hindi, Punjabi, Turkish and Urdu
**AUDIENCE** Parents, women
**PRICE** Free
**PRODUCER** London: Department of Health, 1997
**DISTRIBUTOR** Department of Health Distribution Cente, PO Box 410, Wetherby, West Yorkshire LS23 7LN. Tel: 01937 840250; Fax: 01937 845381

This booklet for pregnant women, originally produced in 1993, contains the most recent advice from the Department of Health about preventing infection from food and from contact with animals.

The booklet identifies some of the infections that can be passed to a pregnant woman through food or contact with animals. The reader is advised about foods to avoid during pregnancy, preparation and cooking methods to minimise the possibility of infection and tips about handling animals and hygiene. It is easy to read and the information is clear with useful checklists at the bottom of each page.

The booklet can stand alone but women may wish to discuss the information with a health professional. Pregnant women and their families will find this a useful and reassuring booklet. It will be of most use if women receive it early in their pregnancy.

# Woman to woman: cervical screening training pack for minority women

**FORMAT** Pack: A4 Ring binder, 75-pages and colour OHTs; A5 photo-story, 38-pages; audio-cassette, 6 min and 36 seconds.
**LANGUAGE** Arabic, African Caribbean (English), Bengali, Cantonese, Mirpuri/Urdu and Vietnamese.
**AUDIENCE** Community health educators and trainers; women from black and minority ethnic groups
**PRICE** £45.00 inc. The photo/audio packs are available separately at £7.50 inc.
**PRODUCER** Rotherham: Rotherham Health Authority, 1998
**DISTRIBUTOR** Rotherham Health Authority Department of Health Promotion, Wharfe Court, Oakwood Hall Drive, Moorgate Road, Rotherham S60 3AQ. Tel: 01709 302094; Fax: 01709 302099

This pack aims to increase the uptake of cervical screening by black and minority ethnic women. It was developed following an action research programme, 'Communicating Breast Screening Messages to Minority Women' in 1993. The pack is primarily written for community health educators and trainers. It should not be used without training.

Much of the core medical and technical content has been simplified to provide a basic understanding for lay people and would therefore probably need supplementing for the training of health professionals.

Part one of the pack is the training handbook, arranged in a number of sections.

The section on 'Reproductive Health and Cervical Screening' covers: the female reproductive system; the menstrual cycle; problems and diseases of the female reproductive system; cervical screening and ethnic minority groups; the smear test; and the cervical screening programme.

The pre-screening education in the 'Community' section looks at: understanding barriers to uptake; the role of the community health educator in the primary care context; understanding ethics in cancer screening education; a code of practice; understanding the role of empowerment in community health education; and intercultural communication in the clinical context.

The next section includes seven workshops covering:
● the role of community health educators in the clinical context;
● facilitating inter-cultural communication in the clinical context;
● exploring risk factors of cervical cancer: cause attribution;
● exploring ethical issues related to cancer screening education;
● the concept of empowerment;
● what's in a word? (this looks at terms that may be used in relation to cervical screening);
● Sughra's smear test experience.

Each workshop sets out the aim and activity. Activities include brainstorming, discussion and role play.

There are five appendices. The first is an outline of a training programme for community educators. The second is an agenda for discussion in a focus group. This includes a series of questions. Appendix three lists 10 general principles of screening, and the fourth appendix is a protocol of 13 basic facts about smear tests. The final appendix, 'Exploring risk factors of cervical cancer-cause attribution', is a press report about a train crash.

The over head transparencies (OHTs) in the 'Resources' section are diagrams of the female reproductive system, the female menstrual cycle, the smear test procedure and managing smear test results.

Part two of the pack comprises an audio-cassette and African–Caribbean photo-story. The cassette is an oral version of the photo-story. These take you through the cervical screening procedure from the invitation letter, through the smear test to receiving the result. A glossary of terms is also provided.

# Women's matters: an introduction to HIV for African women

**FORMAT** Booklet, 28-pages
**LANGUAGE** English
**AUDIENCE** African women affected by HIV
**AUTHOR** H. Massiah and L. Kawonza (ed.)
**PRICE** Single copies free
**PRODUCER** London: Positively Women and Terrence Higgins Trust, 1999 (2nd edition)
**DISTRIBUTOR** The Terrence Higgins Trust, 52-54 Grays Inn Road, London WC1X 8JU. Tel: 0207 831 0330; Fax: 0207 816 4563; Website: www.tht.org.uk

This booklet is for African women living in the UK who are affected by HIV. It discusses various issues related to HIV testing and provides information to help women find out about and access HIV services. The information is interspersed with quotes from HIV positive women about their experiences.

The first part of the booklet explains what HIV and AIDS are, and how HIV is passed on, and discusses HIV testing in detail. In the section on HIV testing, the booklet explores the reasons for testing and emphasises that women have the right to refuse or to ask for pre-test counselling. It explains where women can go for testing, what happens and what a positive result means. The booklet encourages women to seek support, for example from other HIV positive women, their faith or any of the organisations listed. The question of whether to tell people is explored.

Part two is about living with HIV and getting treatments. It provides information about health checks and medical monitoring, and looking after yourself, for example avoiding stress and eating a balanced diet. There is advice on safer sex and relationships. The section on treatments discusses women's rights, and briefly explains combination therapy and the use of complementary therapies. Under 'Pregnancy and children', the booklet raises some issues that HIV-positive women may want to consider before deciding whether to have children, including practical advice about childcare arrangements.

The remainder of the booklet provides information about support services and immigration and welfare benefits. A comprehensive list of services and organisations is provided at the back of the booklet plus details of other publications produced by Terrence Higgins Trust. Some of these are referred to in the text. The booklet was written for the Terrence Higgins Trust and Positively Women in consultation with African women and commissioned by Enfield and Haringey Health Authority on behalf of the Department of Health.

# World of food

**FORMAT** Multimedia pack comprising: work pack, 78-pages, A4 laminated, colour illustrations; teachers notes, 28-pages; A5 recipe booklet with colour photographs, 44-pages; A5 HEA fold-out leaflet, *Enjoy fruit & veg*, illustrated; video, 14 min
**LANGUAGE** English
**AUDIENCE** 8–11-year-olds; 11–14- year-olds, Key Stage 2, Key Stage 3, black and minority ethnic groups
**PRICE** £25.00+£2.00 p&p
**PRODUCER** Bolton: Bolton Community Healthcare, 1994
**DISTRIBUTOR** Food and Health Adviser, Community Healthcare, Bolton, Lever Chambers Centre for Health, Ashburner Street, Bolton BL1 1SQ. Tel: 01204 360094

*World of Food* is a comprehensive food pack designed for use in schools, although it could be used with other groups. The pack was developed following a World Food Festival.

This teaching pack is divided into sections. Section one covers personal stories from Ireland, Africa and the UK. It includes: maps; case studies; questionnaires; and activity sheets. There is also a subsection on the origins of food.

Section 2 includes numerous activity sheets and lesson ideas covering different food groups: enjoy fruit and veg!; starchy staples; meat, fish and beans; daily dairy foods; and snacks.

The third section covers additional topics with activity sheets, information, and labelling ideas. These include: breakfasts around the world; herbs and spices; shopping and markets; and food and festivals.

Additional items in the pack include: hygiene guidelines; a laminated world map; laminated colour photographs; and a contact list that should be adapted for local use.

The 44-page recipe booklet contains 38 recipes from around the world, clearly marked as suitable for either vegetarians or those choosing Halal foods. There are recipes for: starters, snacks and light meals; main meals; accompaniments; desserts; and baking. There is information about the ingredients and where they can be purchased, but this would need to be adapted to reflect the local community.

The video, made in 1993, is less useful than the other parts of the pack. It was made at the World Festival in Bolton and is of variable quality. The video follows participants to the festival venue where they and The Bolton Girls and Lads Brigade prepare a number of dishes, including several recipes from the booklet. The participants include eight groups from the Indian sub-continent, Somalia, Morocco, Bosnia, Burma and Argentina. Explanation is given about how the festival was set up.

## World religions in education 1997/1998 – who am I? The search for individual and group identity

**FORMAT** Journal, 68-pages
**LANGUAGE** English

**AUDIENCE** Teachers
**PRICE** £6.00 inc.
**PRODUCER** London: The Shap Working Party on World Religions in Education, 1998
**DISTRIBUTOR** The Shap Working Party, c/o The National Society's RE Centre, 36 Causton Street, London SW1P 4AU. Tel: 020 7932 1194; Fax: 020 7932 1199; e-mail: nsrec@dial.pipex.com

This journal is for teachers and lecturers of religious education and any one with an interest in this field or working in a multi-racial setting. It is produced by the Shap Working Party on World Religions in Education whose aim is to promote and develop religious education information, materials, resources and training.

The journal contains 11 articles on the theme of identity, religion and culture. They are written by practitioners in the field of religious education and represent a range of organisations and faiths with a contribution from a 12-year-old student writing about her experiences as a young Muslim woman.

The articles look at identity in its widest context covering a range of issues: national and European issues; working with students in the Hindu community; working with student teachers and students with learning difficulties. There is also an article on mentoring student teachers. The articles are informative with examples of good practice.

The journal reviews new publications aimed at Key Stages 1-3 and includes a list of current Shap publications.

## Young and equal. A standard for racial equality in services working with young people

**FORMAT** Pack, 33-pages
**LANGUAGE** English
**AUDIENCE** Purchasers and providers of services for young people
**PRICE** £5.00+10% p&p
**PRODUCER** London: Commission for Racial Equality, 1995
**DISTRIBUTOR** Central Books, 99 Wallis Road, London E9 5LN.
Tel: 020 8986 5488; Fax: 020 8533 5821; e-mail peter@centbks.demon.co.uk

This pack is for anyone who works with young people. It aims to enable organisations to review their current practice and to identify action for achieving racial equality in service delivery. The Standard for Racial Equality draws on the Statement of Purpose for youth work agreed by the National Youth Agency in 1992. The pack was produced by the Commission for Racial Equality but includes comments and advice from individuals and other organisations.

The pack is divided into five sections: Introduction; The case for action – the 'quality' case for racial equality and putting into practice the Statement of Purpose; The legal case – Race Relations Act 1976; Setting the standard – policy and planning, services for young people, recruitment and selection of staff, developing and retaining staff. The final section includes five action levels through which racial equality can be achieved. Working through these levels will enable organisations to establish the level appropriate for them. There are outcomes and indicators in each section so that progress can be measured.

Organisations will find this a useful tool for developing policy at all levels. It could be used as part of a long-term organisational development or action plan. However, there are resource and financial implications when implementing the standards. For example, training for workers and managers, time for consultation with users, the local community or other groups and for monitoring and review.

## Your drink and you

**FORMAT** Booklet 16-pages, illustrated
**LANGUAGE** English for African–Caribbean audience
**AUDIENCE** African–Caribbean public
**PRICE** Free
**PRODUCER** London: Health Education Authority, 1998
**DISTRIBUTOR** HEA Customer Services, Marston Book Services, PO Box 269, Abingdon, Oxon OX14 4YN.
Tel: 01235 465565/6; Fax: 01235 465556

This booklet about alcohol and drinking is aimed at a general African–Caribbean audience. It explains what sensible drinking means in terms of the recommended daily benchmarks for men and women. This includes an explanation of the 'unit' system for measuring the strength of different alcoholic drinks.

The booklet covers the risks to health from drinking too much and counters some of the misconceptions about alcohol in a section on myths and facts. There are brief sections on alcohol and the family, alcohol and medication, alcohol, anxiety and depression, alcohol and sickle cell disorder and drinking and pregnancy.
At the back of the booklet are some helpful tips on sensible drinking and useful telephone helpline numbers.

# Appendix 1
# Reviewers and critical readers

## Reviewers

The HEA would like to thank the following reviewers for their contribution to the database and directory.

### Original reviews
Mary Ryan, Health Promotion Information Centre, HEA

### Ongoing reviews
Noreen Howard
Julie Griffith
Yvonne Field
Lesley de Meza

## Critical readers

The following critical readers contributed to the development of the original health-related resources database for black and minority ethnic groups by commenting on a number of the initial reviews and the HEA would like to thank them for their expert guidance.

Fauzia Ahmad
Health Promotion Officer, Lewisham and North Southwark Health Promotion Unit

Pami Bal
Project Manager, Staff Training and Development Centre, North Mersey Community NHS Trust

Rose Das
Health Adviser, GUM Clinic, Newcastle General Hospital

Poonam Jagota
Project Worker, South Manchester Health Promotion Unit

Kiran Kumar
Senior Health Promotion Officer, North Bedfordshire Health Promotion Unit

Ziba Nadimi
Health Promotion Officer, East London and the City Health Promotion Service

Frances Presley
Information Officer, SHARE, King's Fund Centre

Kirat Randhawa
Trainee Health Promotion Officer, Camden and Islington Health Promotion Unit

Phil Sealy and the staff of Standing Conference of Ethnic Minority Senior Citizens (SCEMSC)

Ghulam Shabbir
Environmental Health Officer, Environmental Health/Road Safety Department, Cambridgeshire County Council

Gulab Singh
Deputy District Health Promotion Officer, Preston Health Promotion Unit

# Appendix 2
# Directories of black and minority ethnic initiatives and resources

## *Directory of African Caribbean Initiatives.* Department of Health, 1998.

A directory of initiatives and resources that address the cultural and linguistic needs of the African–Caribbean communities. It is divided into nine sections: Books and booklets; Catalogues; Conferences; Leaflets; Projects; Reports; Service provision; Training resource and Videos. Each entry includes a brief description of the initiative and provides contact details.

Price: £14.95 (health authorities); free (voluntary groups)
Distributor: N Films, 78 Holyhead Road, Handsworth, Birmingham B21 0LH

## *Directory of Asian Initiatives.* Department of Health, 1998.

A directory in Hindi, Bengali, English, Gujerati, Punjabi and Urdu of initiatives and resources that address the cultural and linguistic needs of the Asian communities. It is divided into 13 sections: Introduction; Accident prevention and first aid; Commercial and TV fillers and TV programmes; Complementary medicine; Diseases and illnesses; Drugs, Alcohol, Tobacco and Paan; General health; Heart disease; Mental health; Pregnancy, childbirth and childcare; Patient information; Radio programmes; and Women's health. Each entry includes a brief description and provides contact details.

Price: £14.95 (health authorities); free (voluntary groups)
Distributor: N Films, 78 Holyhead Road, Handsworth, Birmingham B21 0LH

# *Directory of Ethnic Minority Initiatives*, Volume 2. Department of Health, 1998.

The second edition of a directory of projects addressing black and minority ethnic health commissioned between April 1993 and March 1996. There are projects on primary care, purchaser development, the patient's charter and inequalities in health, plus specific medical conditions or aspects of health. The projects range from the production of leaflets to more long- term development work. The directory is divided into five sections: Patient's Charter; Health of the Nation; NHS reforms and purchaser development; Voluntary sector development; and Primary care-led NHS. Each entry includes a brief description and provides contact details.

Price: free
Distributor: Department of Health Distribution Centre, P O Box 410, Wetherby, West Yorkshire LS23 7LN